THE ANCESTORS

VOLUME 2

JEAN BOVELL

Published by BookPublishingWorld in 2018

Copyright © Jean Bovell, 2018

The right of Jean Bovell to be identified as Author of this work has been asserted in accordance with sections 77 and 78 of the Copyright, Designs and Patents Act, 1988.

No part of this book is to be reproduced, reprinted, copied, or stored in retrieval systems of any type, except by written permission from the Author. Parts of this book may, however, be used only in reference to support-related documents.

All rights reserved. A CIP catalogue record for this book is available from the British Library.

ISBN: 978-1-911412-75-5

BookPublishingWorld
An imprint of Dolman Scott
www.dolmanscott.com

THE ANCESTORS
VOLUME 2

THE ANCESTORS VOLUME 2, is being written in response to the numerous requests for a second volume of the true-life historical story, THE ANCESTORS. There was a general hunger for "more". Readers had been fascinated by the humorous and intriguing saga relating to the childhood adventures of the surviving offspring of William and Angie Radix that was concluded in summaries relating to their separate choices in adult life. But this resulted in a general feeling of being left hanging and lingering curiosity in relation to how the lives of these remarkable individuals may have unfolded.

Chronicled with significant historical events, THE ANCESTORS featured the unique experiences of three generations of single-minded, self-empowering first daughters who lived on a small Caribbean island during the nineteenth and twentieth centuries.

The first of the three matriarchs had been given the name Hope, reflective of being the first child within her community to be born into freedom following the abolition of slavery. Hope, in due course, developed into an intelligent young woman with a strong sense of self-worth and an all-consuming determination to break the cycle of being just another "taken for granted" oppressed and subservient wife and mother, which had been the accepted norm for females in her community of the era. In her quest for realising her dream of a life of liberty and independence, Hope boldly abandoned her husband and older children. She fled to the island of Trinidad, accompanied only by her newly born baby daughter.

Hope went on to achieve the self-control she craved, but even though she did not return to the island of her birth, she was happy to have re-established contact with the siblings left behind. She was also delighted when the baby girl in her care grew into a beautiful young lady and married a man with "prospects". Although Hope never doubted that she had made the right decision by seeking a better life abroad, the abandonment of her children had been emotionally costly, and she remained haunted by the guilt of putting her personal aspirations before the parental needs of her children. Hope was, however, heartened when, in subsequent years, several of her descendants followed in their grandmother's footsteps by deciding to embark on a new life on the relatively prosperous island of Trinidad. Indeed, there is to this day a flourishing family network of Hope's descendants who reside within the suburb of Diego Martin in the city of Port-of-Spain, Trinidad.

Back home, Hope's first daughter, Dee-Dee, had given birth to her very own first daughter, Angie. The child was born out of wedlock, but Dee-Dee went on to meet and marry a wealthy landowner by the name of Way Lett. Of the couple's eight children who had not travelled abroad in adult life, several carried on the tradition of productive land-ownership or thrived in their individual career choices.

Dee-Dee's first-born, Angie Telesford, was the last in line of the trio of first daughters, and she became the teenage bride of William Radix. The couple created fourteen children, twelve of whom survived.

THE ANCESTORS profiled the contrasting parenting styles of an easy-going and nurturing father and controlling and domineering mother, intent on keeping the siblings on a tight rein.

Although she may have been considered a domestic tyrant, Angie was at the same time self-less and philanthropic, and in various ways provided a valuable service of care within her local community. William, on the other hand, focused on his business ventures, but the education of his offspring had been a crucial priority. He ensured they received access to the best learning opportunities that were available to them and monitored their progress.

The different methods and personalities of two devoted parents would undoubtedly have influenced the specific calling and altruistic pursuits of various members of the clan. This continued biopic showcases their shared joviality and sense of fun, alongside melancholic, addictive or reclusive tendencies. But this particular band of brothers and sisters, who had rarely been permitted to mingle outdoors with other children, clung to each other and were like one. They remained tightly bonded and at all times supportive of each other throughout their separate eventful life journeys.

This narrative offers an insight into the hearts and minds of a family from a bygone age who lived in a society that was deeply divided between the haves and have nots. But they emerged as pioneers during a period when professional practitioner positions in Law, Medicine and Dentistry had been exclusively the domain of white British men.

THE ANCESTORS VOLUME 2, offers a heart-felt and graphic portrayal of separate experiences of love, betrayal, success, tragedy and loss. This compilation of true-life stories is interspersed with historical political affiliations.

Jean Bovell

The Author would like to thank the descendants of our subjects and persons noted in separate stories, for their valuable contributions.

"They were a strange lot," said many.

Names are withheld within the narrative in cases where anonymity has been requested.

Historical records accessed from the Grenada National Museum. Established in 1976.

CONTENTS

THE HEART BENEATH 3

SHATTERED DREAMS 19

BEST THINGS IN LIFE ARE FREE 43

LONE STAR 53

ESSENTIALLY GRASSROOTS 61

SEIZE THE MOMENT 71

A TALE OF TWO SISTERS 83

BELIEVE AND ACHIEVE 109

YOU LIVE ONLY ONCE 121

UNPRECIDENTED 135

PRINCIPLED MAN 149

THE HEART BENEATH

The 1960s had been the decade that heralded in significant first-time events on the tri-island state of Grenada, Carriacou and Petite Martinique. Amongst these were the establishment of the Grenada Teachers' College in 1963 and Gloria St Bernard being elected first female mayor for the city of St George the following year. Queen Elizabeth II was welcomed on her first State visit to the island in 1966. Eric Gairy was elected the first Grenadian-born Prime Minister in 1967. And in 1968, Mrs Hilda Bynoe, a medical doctor, was made the first home-grown Governor of the tri-island state. She was also the first female to have held the prestigious position. All the while, the country as a whole was being steadily modernised, but the extension of electricity from Grenville to Sauteurs in 1966 had been a long-awaited and much-needed life-enhancing resource.

Although the curtailing of migrants to the United Kingdom from 1962 may have been disappointing to some, it was counter-balanced by an increase in the number of families and individuals permitted to enter the United States.

The nineteen sixties had been, essentially, an optimistic period, when nationalism and patriotism were generated and celebrated.

And so, it was, on a particular sunny morning during the latter years of the "feel-good" decade, an attractive middle-aged woman called Clarice glowed with serenity and a deep sense of peace as she made her way home from Sunday Mass. Consumed by a surge of spiritual rejuvenation, Clarice could not help but hum the chorus of the closing hymn and, with a toss of her head, burst tunefully into the final verse. All the while, her cheeks were being caressed by the cool and soothing morning breeze that accompanied the heat of the morning sun. Clarice thanked God for his blessings and pledged that she would, as always, strive to "do good". Little did she know that the promise of a glorious day ahead was about to be broken and would ultimately lead to tragedy.

On arrival at the house divided into two separate apartments that was shared with her brother O'Hanley, joyful feelings were suddenly replaced by anger and frustration. Clarice found herself being confronted by an inebriated and bedraggled-looking housemate, tightly clutching the rail that surrounded the porch of his upper-floor dwelling and swaying from side to side as he struggled to stay on his feet. Clarice was livid. How could he be drunk so early in the morning? It was only 9.00am. Furthermore, Sunday should be a Holy Day of rest and reflection. It was all too much. Clarice let rip, and, in angry and forceful tones, orchestrated by a gesticulating clenched fist, roared: "O'Hanley! This drinking must STOP! You can't carry on like this. IT MUST STOP!"

O'Hanley doggedly refused to be bowed. Who does Clarice think she is, he may have thought, making demands about how "I should live my life"? His response was equally confrontational and robust. "I WON'T STOP! I REFUSE TO STOP!"

Consumed with profound exasperation by her brother's wilful stance, Clarice angrily stomped into her ground-floor apartment and recalled, with a large degree of despondency, the childhood challenges that had been presented by her younger brother. O'Hanley had been the rebellious child in the family and, as a consequence, endured frequent severe beatings from their tyrannical mother. Only their lovingly measured father showed any compassion or understanding into the possible underlying causes of his son's disturbing behavioural patterns. However, on that particular Sunday morning, any idea that O'Hanley may have been in need of some form of help with overcoming his alcohol addiction would not have entered Clarice's psyche, as she threw her hands up in despair. That man would never change, she told herself; but on regaining her composure, she offered a prayer and hoped for spiritual intervention.

A few days following their Sunday altercation, Clarice became increasingly concerned that she had not seen or heard from O'Hanley for several days. Despite their different lifestyles, Clarice maintained interest in her brother's well-being and never failed to be reassured on seeing him leaving or entering his apartment. O'Hanley, on his part, would call in on his sister when sober. The pair would invariably exchange pleasantries, and O'Hanley was at all times appreciative of the cooked meal that was reliably on offer from his older sibling.

After three days of having no sight or sound of her brother, Clarice decided to investigate; but it was with a heavy sense of foreboding that she cautiously entered his apartment. "O'Hanley! O'Hanley! O'Hanley!" bellowed Clarice, while walking through the various rooms. Suddenly, she stumbled into something on the floor and, as she steadied herself after almost losing her balance, looked down to find O'Hanley lying motionless at her feet. Clarice gasped, dropped to her knees in shock and proceeded to check her brother for any life responses. There was none and, moreover, his body was alarmingly icy cold. "Oh, my God. He is GONE!" Clarice exclaimed. Agitated and overcome by an extreme state of panic, she hurried down the stairs and into the street, screaming hysterically, "Help! Help! Help!"

On hearing her cries, neighbours and passers-by quickly ran to Clarice's side. Shocked by her unbelievable outpourings, the emergency services were immediately alerted and close family members were informed. Within minutes, bells sounded as police and ambulance dashed to the scene. Paramedics wasted no time in initiating resuscitation procedures, but it would be to no avail. O'Hanley was pronounced dead at the scene.

Clarice and her surviving brothers comforted each other as they reeled in stunned disbelief. The small inquisitive crowd that had gathered outside the house were also staggered, and it was not long before news of the tragedy was spread like wildfire throughout the town community.

Due to the unexplained circumstances surrounding O'Hanley's demise, an autopsy examination was undertaken. It was determined that O'Hanley had lost his life from a bleed on the brain after falling and hitting his head whilst being under the influence of alcohol. Clarice could not help but recollect, with regret, the last heated dialogue held with her brother. If only she had ignored his demeanour, which would no doubt have resulted in their last encounter being congenial. Clarice also wondered whether she had in some way failed her brother by not checking on him sooner, or possibly doing more to help him. Indeed, various other members of the sibling group lamenting O'Hanley's untimely passing may have fostered similar regrets regarding their dishevelled and disorderly, albeit warm-hearted brother who had lost direction in life.

O'Hanley's funeral had been well attended and included friends and locals who knew him well. But as visibly distressed close family members agonised at the graveside over the sad and untimely loss, the importance of being kind regardless of a person's status, lifestyle or how they presented may have resonated, particularly with the nieces and nephews who had been intolerant of their vagrant uncle. No doubting O'Hanley would have been heartened that it was being reaffirmed at his farewell gathering that he was, without question, a full-blooded and accepted member of the family fold. Not just a "rogue", as he had grown accustomed to being called; but more of a "loveable rogue". It was also a time when the siblings may have reflected on how O'Hanley "stepped up to the plate" when he willingly boosted the family income by working alongside their father and brother, in a foreign land, during a period when the once relatively prosperous family had been experiencing hardship.

O'Hanley was the sixth offspring, which included one set of twins, produced by William and Angie Radix within the first five years of their marriage. The young mother, just 22 years of age when she gave birth to O'Hanley, was undoubtedly overwhelmed and at a stage where the seeds of disgruntlement were being sewn regarding the perpetual arrival of babies. William and Angie were a happily married couple and shared a loving and passionate relationship. But at a time when contraception had been largely inaccessible to those who resided on English-speaking Caribbean islands, large families were generally accepted as being part and parcel of married life.

During the early years of the 20th century, and in their particular culture, mothers held day-to-day responsibility for the disciplining of children. Angie could have been considered a merciless disciplinarian, as her children were regularly reduced to whimpering heaps of bruised flesh, inflicted by the whip for the smallest misdemeanour. But while his siblings cowered in the presence of their mother or endeavoured to avoid her wrath by bowing to her demands, O'Hanley remained defiant. He was, as a consequence, regularly severely chastised for being defiant. The resulting build-up of frustration would usually be played out at school, where he released his anger by attacking female teachers.

Despite the presented challenges, O'Hanley responded well to the praise he received from his father, William, for the smallest achievement, and was always better behaved whenever his elder was around. William disapproved of Angie's treatment of their son and urged an alternative approach that included a little kindness and recognition of the things he did well. O'Hanley was judged by his father to be a sensitive soul, in spite of his deviant behaviours, and needed to feel loved by his mother. However, it was not to be. Children in those days were expected to be at all times submissive and respectful in the presence of adults, and in particular those in authority. As a consequence, Angie placed full blame on O'Hanley for daring, even contemplating, challenging her rightful authority. However, she did consider the possibility that her son's behaviour may have been the result of a brain injury caused by the large coconut that fell off the tree and landed heavily on his head when he was just a small boy.

Although corporal punishment was commonly used on children of the era, the particular community had no idea of the concept that related to "child abuse". And discipline was delivered in isolation of the overall care provided. In line with his brothers and sisters, O'Hanley had been a healthily nourished and well-dressed child; and, when calm, a capable student at school. He was never excluded from planned family activities, maintained a close relationship with his siblings and harboured a secure sense of belonging. Angie kept the little ones on a tight rein. They were, in the main, allowed outdoors only when they were sent to school, church, clubs or on specific errands. This resulted in the children spending much of their time in each other's company. They clung together and a firm sibling bond was developed between them. Despite these factors, the children did receive "time out" for a few short hours on Sunday afternoons, when they were free to pursue their separate interests. O'Hanley often spent his personal time indulging hobbies in fishing, hunting for wild game or playing cricket or marbles with other boys in the community.

The intelligent and single-minded youngster developed into a strong and strapping teenager. Consequently, when difficulties beckoned and William had no option but to close his once lucrative business and seek employment overseas, O'Hanley was selected, along with older brother Lloyd, to accompany their father. It was intended that the three men would work alongside each other and that their combined income would serve to bolster the family's financial circumstances. O'Hanley was delighted that he was picked, and the feeling of validation that had been a long time coming was immense. Furthermore, the prospect of living apart from his draconian mother and being with the father he adored and with whom he was at ease, transcended into absolute euphoria. O'Hanley would not be disappointed: the experience of working abroad with his father and brother proved to be, at that point, the happiest period in his life. But no-one knows what tomorrow may bring.

The work plan that had been put into action was having the desired positive effect on the family's overall income. It was expected to continue until such time that the economic climate in the homeland improved, thus enabling William to restart his business. Unfortunately, it was not to be. Unexpectedly, and without warning, William contracted an illness that lingered and the men were unanimous in their decision that William should seek healing and recuperation at home. The trio was optimistic and shared the view that within weeks William would have returned to his usual robust health and that they would resume their employment abroad. But William unexpectedly succumbed to the symptoms of an undiagnosed illness within a fortnight. He was just 49 years of age. The family was shocked and shattered. The demise of the main breadwinner signalled a significant turning point in the lives of those left behind.

The time spent working abroad proved satisfyingly liberating for O'Hanley. He had tasted independence and it was sweet. He proved himself to be a physically resilient young man who tackled manual work with enthusiasm. The incentive was being rewarded with a lucrative salary. O'Hanley made a decision. He boarded a ship and headed for Columbia, albeit with a mournful heart over the loss of his father. He was not, however, sad to be parted from his sometime stern and authoritarian mother. O'Hanley would subsequently cut off all contact with his family and create a life of his choosing in various countries within South America.

Although O'Hanley had been singled out as being the problematic son, Angie became increasingly concerned that nothing had been heard from him over the ensuing years. She worried that he may have come to harm and prayed each day for his safety. Angie hoped that she would one day receive a letter from her errant son, but it was never to be. Not knowing whether O'Hanley was dead or alive had been an agonising thorn which persisted until Angie's passing, twenty-two years after his departure. It seemed that in one way or the other and throughout his life, O'Hanley presented challenges to his mother. Moreover, the family were saddened that, because of their brother's unknown whereabouts, he could not be informed of Angie's final illness and subsequent death.

Many years passed and memories of O'Hanley had to a large degree faded from the consciousness of many when, out of the blue, he appeared. O'Hanley had decided to return home for good. He longed to be back in the community where he grew up and be with his family again. In particular, O'Hanley felt a desperate need to see his mother and felt that she should be the first family member to know that he was back. And, filled with anticipation at the prospect of catching her unawares and carrying gifts, O'Hanley headed for the family home in Vincennes, situated in the parish of St. David. He could hardly wait! But his joyful expression faded and confusion took over when he arrived to find an empty house.

As O'Hanley stood bewildered in front of the building that was once home, a neighbour appeared. The elderly gentleman nodded, delivered a polite greeting and, without a question being asked, proceeded to talk about the past occupants of the house. O'Hanley was shocked and visibly shaken on being told that the people had packed up and moved to the city of St. George and that the matriarch, Mrs Radix, passed away several years subsequently. The planned wonderful surprise now lay in tatters. It had been a gut-wrenching disappointment. O'Hanley was consumed with feelings of regret that he had not maintained contact with his mother. He wondered whether he had been naïve in assuming that she would always be there, or had he simply overlooked the briefness of time?

O'Hanley stared in total disbelief at the abandoned "shell" which had been for so many years the family home. So full of life. A bustling environment filled with different personalities whose commonality had been shared feelings of belonging, security and stability. He was now faced with a soul-less structure of bricks and mortar. It had been a moment of stark awakening. All that remained now were cherished memories. New and on-coming generations would undoubtedly be oblivious of the building's "once upon a time" spirited occupiers.

It was with a heavy heart that O'Hanley then visited his brothers Daniel and Ivan, who continued to reside within the parish. The men were overwhelmed to see O'Hanley again after so many years and embraced him warmly, quickly followed by offerings of food and drink. Despite the lengthy separation, there had been no slackening of sibling ties. They simply picked up again, with conversations that were relaxed and free-flowing, and O'Hanley received first-hand knowledge relating to their mother's passing following a short illness. But there were also recollections of happy times spent as children and their shared humour was reflected in spontaneous hearty laughter.

After a few days spent with his brothers and visiting with old friends and close relatives such as the Letts, O'Hanley travelled to the city of St George and presented at the homes of the siblings who resided in the locality. They also were thrilled to see their long-lost but not forgotten sibling and a very happy reunion followed. O'Hanley would in time reveal his desire to settle among the town community. However, he had returned to the homeland with very little money and was, as a consequence, unable to afford a place of his own. The family were concerned and rallied to help their sibling. O'Hanley received rent-free accommodation from John, who also never hesitated to provide financial assistance whenever it became necessary. Lloyd, on the other hand, ensured that O'Hanley earned every penny by providing him with employment, which included working the land during the planting and reaping seasons. O'Hanley spent the majority of his spare time fishing, and additional income would come from selling the majority of the day's catch. After over thirty years spent working in various South American countries, the pressure was off. O'Hanley was now semi-retired and enjoying a less arduous lifestyle and being in regular contact with his family.

O'Hanley was a warm-hearted, care-free and jovial soul, who harboured no qualms about being dependent on the family for his livelihood. Despite being stubbornly insistent on living life his way, he was harmless, presented no challenges and was never involved with the law. Apart from fishing, O'Hanley loved women and "drinking rum" and indulged them both in local clubs or bars at weekends. It was on one of these jaunts that he met and formed a friendship with an attractive young lady. The friendship developed into a relationship and it was not long before the love interest had been invited to share O'Hanley's apartment. Everyone was pleased that O'Hanley had settled into what, at face value, appeared a committed relationship. The couple, in time, produced a son, and O'Hanley was proved a doting dad. Unlike his own upbringing, he ensured that corporal punishment would never be a discipline option and modelled his parenting on his father's methods.

O'Hanley was fairly successful in maintaining stability in his personal life and daily family routines seemed to be moving along smoothly. Even so, he would on occasions become bored with the doldrum that often comes with domesticity. It was during those "down times" that O'Hanley strayed from the straight and narrow and rejuvenated his love life by sneaking into secret casual affairs with a variety of girls, ready and willing to exchange sexual favours for money, gifts or even a measure of rum!

O'Hanley loved all children and was friendly and playful in his interactions with them. In particular, he had been keenly interested in the welfare of his young nieces and nephews and would enquire into how they were doing. Thirteen-year-old Michael recalled "Uncle O'Hanley" commenting on how much he had grown, before asking the question: "Have you had a woman yet?"

"No," Michael replied promptly.

"What! No woman yet?" uncle retorted in mocked shocked tones and humorously added: "Don't worry, leave it with me. I'll fix you up."

The innocent boy was left feeling confused but curious. "What did uncle mean when he said that he would 'fix me up'?" he wondered but recollected that the older man had indicated that he was "only joking". But Michael would soon discover that it was no joke when he was spirited away by his uncle, and found himself alone, in the presence of a naked woman, old enough to be his mother! Within minutes, the bewildered youngster was helpless in resisting being seduced by the seasoned practitioner. The moments of pleasurable discovery that ensued were never forgotten.

Time marched on, but O'Hanley never regretted his decision to return home after many years living and working abroad. Life was good. His relationship had been progressing satisfactorily. He was enjoying fatherhood, and the support he received from his siblings remained solid. Over time, O'Hanley had become a well-known and popular figure around the town and was given the nickname "Boss", indicative of being a popular and much-liked member of the local community. Children loved their older friend and, with his own son in tow, O'Hanley would join in with their games, tell jokes and distribute bags of home-made boiled candy.

At the time that sister, Clarice, returned to the homeland after a period of stay in the United States, O'Hanley had already separated from his partner. He did not, however, lose contact with the couple's son, who remained in the care of his mother. It was at this point that Clarice stepped in and offered support by inviting O'Hanley to share her house by occupying the upper-floor of the building. There was general concern within the family circle that O'Hanley may have lost his way. He often appeared unwashed, dishevelled and "drunk", and was frequently likened to a "vagrant". It was now hoped that the much-loved and respected older sister would be influential in bringing about the desired changes in a man who had descended into a chaotic lifestyle.

Even though Clarice was, during the period, looking after elderly aunt, Evie, with whom she shared living space, no stone was left unturned in her efforts to help her brother. It was, however, to no avail. O'Hanley stubbornly refused to co-operate and continued on his self-destructive path. Nonetheless, family support did not falter. O'Hanley received financial assistance from his brothers, and there was always a cooked meal on offer from Clarice. But, on observing O'Hanley entering or exiting his apartment, Clarice would sigh with relief and utter the words: "At least he's still alive – Thank God."

O'Hanley's down-hill slide began following the collapse of his relationship. He fell apart, sank into depression, abandoned work and, by so doing, lost all motivation and purpose. By the time of his passing, he had descended into a sad, lonely and reclusive existence. He missed having the comfort and tender loving care of his female companion and increasingly found solace in the bottle. He died alone, following a fall. There was no-one present to offer a helping hand. Clarice's sense of relief that her brother was "still alive" on seeing him on a daily basis, may have been premonition of his tragic end. But her sense of foreboding on entering O'Hanley's apartment on that fateful day had been disturbingly overwhelming.

At a time when children were expected to be seen and not heard, O'Hanley's headstrong character had been quite extraordinary. Unlike his siblings, who toed the line or may have invented strategies for avoiding the wrath of their mother, O'Hanley remained fearlessly defiant, in spite of the harsh consequences. His anger may have been rooted in the perceived mistreatment he received from her, but solace was always at hand from a father who had been consistently nurturing, sympathetic and understanding.

Although O'Hanley was fundamentally a proud man who insisted on living life his way, he may nonetheless have learnt lessons from the ordeal he endured as a growing boy. He was, as an adult, never physical in his responses to acrimonious situations and was essentially harmless, in spite of being robustly stubborn in his interactions. However, beneath it all was a caring and sensitive heart who needed to feel accepted and valued.

O'Hanley is remembered fondly by close family members and those who knew him well.

O'Hanley Radix
1907 - 1968

SHATTERED DREAMS

When asked to comment on the life of his mother, Walter, son of Clarice, reflected on the life experiences of his beloved mother with pensive expression and sighed despondently. "She had a hard life," he replied. His demeanour indicated that it had been much too painful to go into detail, but in melancholy tones, repeated: "She had a hard life." He went no further.

Clarice, who was the second offspring and first daughter born to William and Angie Radix, first experienced trauma as a three-year-old toddler. Her twin Iris had died suddenly and the loss of her favourite playmate left the little girl shattered and confused. Despite being comforted by her parents and told that Iris had gone to heaven to be with "the Angels", it was no consolation to this little girl. Clarice was unable to understand why Iris did not take her with him when he went to play with "the Angels" in heaven and felt that she had been abandoned by her very best friend. She was, as a consequence, totally bereft.

Although memories of the lost brother would be forever imprinted onto the memory, Clarice grew into a vivacious, confident and popular young girl. She was a much-loved daughter and sister who had been in the privileged position of being the only girl among six boys for a considerable period. Not surprisingly, Clarice may have revelled in being the spoilt centre of attraction. Even the maternal disciplinarian harboured a "soft spot" for her special little girl and encouraged her hobbies in baking and jam-making. Clarice was also dressed in the latest fashion of the day and even her underwear had been colourful and skilfully embroidered. Clarice excelled in her school work and was judged to be brainier than her siblings. She was rewarded for her exemplary academic performance by being presented with a grand piano by her proud father and went on to become an enthusiastic student of music. In spite of her advantaged upbringing, Clarice remained unspoilt. She was a delightful personality: caring, considerate and helpful to others.

Clarice's school career ended with examination results that indicated top marks in all subjects taken. William and Angie were elated. Consequently, when Clarice expressed the desire to study for a career in the United States, the couple did not hesitate in providing encouragement and support. They were hopeful that their beautiful, conscientious and intelligent daughter would be successful in her chosen career, but most of all prayed for her personal happiness. In those days, a girl or woman was considered "lucky" if she bagged herself a good husband. It had been William and Angie's priority wish for their treasured daughter.

It was with her parents' blessings that Clarice headed for the United States. Apart from the trauma suffered following the tragic loss of her twin brother, Iris, Clarice's childhood journey had been filled with happiness. But she was now entering a new chapter as an independent young lady in a foreign country. Clarice knew that she would have to work and study hard if she were to realise her career goal and was prepared to knuckle down to the tasks that lay ahead. She was determined to do well, but above all, wanted to make her parents, William and Angie, proud. Nothing at that juncture could have clouded her "rose-coloured" view of the future. She reflected on her childhood experiences of being raised together with her brothers and sisters by a devoted couple and within a stable and secure environment. And for many years holding the favoured position of being the much-loved only daughter, and sole sister among six brothers. In spite of having to cope with the loss of her twin, Clarice's life experience as a child and young adult had been undeniably idyllic. Even though she was sad to leave her family behind, she could not help being filled with a keen sense of optimism as she anticipated the bright future that lay head.

On arrival in the big city of New York, Clarice felt that she had entered into a completely new world. It had been, for her, an unexpected and stunning cultural shock. In contrast to the small, rural and sleepy community from whence she came, Clarice now found herself in a modern and fast-moving place where everything, including roads and buildings, was so much larger. Although not integrated, New York was at the time a diverse city where people from separate communities, including Irish, Italian, Jewish and West Indian, could be seen bustling about their business. Numerous buses and motor-cars of similar make, colour and design chugged noisily along huge roads. Children ran and played freely on wide sidewalks lined with retail outlets, while pedestrians hurried about their business, crossing over streets by fearlessly stepping into moving traffic. In due course, Clarice would be made aware of previously unheard of, modern technologies such as radio, cinema, telephones, running water and electric lights.

Climate change had also been a first-time experience for Clarice. She loved the fluffy softness of fresh snow but found the hot humid nights during the summer months quite unbearable.

Clarice landed in New York during one of the most notably historic decades of the 20th century. It was the early nineteen twenties, an era in which tolerance reigned. Differences were respected or even celebrated. Opportunities were available to all, and individuals felt confidently emboldened by the "feel good" inclusive environment in which they lived. Moreover, it was a time when women in general had been victorious, having being for the first time given the right to vote. It was also the period, after World War I, when many African-American artists, writers and political activists, who campaigned for the "advancement" of coloured people, moved from the segregated South to the more liberal North. These progressive and talented individuals settled in a large black neighbourhood within the borough of Manhattan, known as Harlem. They were joined by their jazz musician contemporaries from New Orleans, a city known for its musical creativity and culture. It seemed that these emigrant musicians carried with them the spirit of the Southern City, as Harlem became the heartbeat and most famous hub of entertainment, celebrated for introducing an original "rip-roaring" sound. The new musical genre, known as "jazz", would be wholeheartedly embraced and duplicated, not only in New York but throughout the nation and worldwide. The era was termed "the Jazz age". A time when various young New Yorkers of all races and social classes flocked to Harlem's speakeasies, bars, ballrooms and theatres for a night of exciting entertainment. Revellers of the day would frantically and merrily dance to pulsating rhythms played-out by slide pianists or live jazz bands. The electrifying environment was fuelled by free-flowing liquor, banned by law, but supplied undercover and controlled by organised crime. The risk of collectively participating in an illegal activity would no doubt have promoted consumption and infused a thrilling element to the overall climate of euphoria.

The 1920s decade had also been the age of the silent movie, and individuals flocked in large numbers to see the latest releases. Movie fans particularly loved comedy shorts, with fast-moving and hilarious themes that featured the most popular comedians of the period. It was, overall, an exciting and exhilarating experience to be alive, young and living in the city of New York.

Although she was, at the time, in a world filled with entertainment and good times, Clarice was among many who, for a variety of reasons, were not involved in the party scene. However, they may have read about it in newspapers or, like Clarice, simply watched from the side-lines. Clarice would hold her breath in awe whenever she encountered beautifully attired young men and women setting out on an evening of jollies. Clarice had been a fashionable "trend-setter" within the small community from which she hailed, but these New York designs had been, in her mind, "something else". The female trend-setters of the day, known as "It Girls", were particularly impressive. They would step out in stockinged feet and pointed high-heel shoes. Their short and waved hairstyles were often adorned with feathers attached to colourful bandeaus or covered with pretty little caps that caressed thickly powdered faces and bright red lips. The dresses worn may be short, mid-length or long, but all with distinctively patterned hemlines and accessorised with various combinations of outlandish eye-catching jewellery.

Commonly known as "flappers", modern-day party girls may be accompanied by sharply attired young men in white suits with matching shirts and ties. Checked suits with bow ties. Or a black and white ensemble. But the long silk scarves, stylish statement hats and classy two-tone shoes had been the finishing touches to an overall appearance that engendered swank and swagger.

It had been indeed a deliciously feel-good, altruistic era that nurtured equality, enabled minorities and collectively waved the freedom flag. It was, as a consequence, wonderfully liberating to be young, to be a woman and to be black. What better time for Clarice to be in New York? Her positive view of the future had been endorsed by being a fully-fledged member of this new generation who were convinced that the good times would roll on forever.

There had been no shortage of jobs, and it was not long before Clarice found employment as a live-in Domestic Assistant at the home of a well-to-do "Jewish" family who resided in a pleasant suburb within the city. Clarice had been staying, on a temporary basis, with a middle-aged couple from the homeland. The couple had emigrated to the US after World War I, a period when the United States Government had, for the first time, opened the door to West Indian migrants. Clarice was delighted. She had at last found her feet. The live-in position had been most beneficial. It guaranteed not only a regular income, but also incorporated rent-free accommodation. Furthermore, her employers expressed support in relation to her educational aspirations and agreed to enable additional free periods when required.

The garden could not have appeared rosier at the time that Clarice waved goodbye to the kindly people with whom she lived and moved into the home of her new employers. Not long afterwards, Clarice enrolled into evening classes and began combining work with study. She had begun the process that should eventually lead to a worthwhile career. Everything was, so far, going to plan, and she was happy. In the meantime, family contact was being maintained via letter-writing. Clarice needed the emotional reassurances of the folk back home, and they were relieved to hear that she had adjusted to her new life in New York and was doing well.

Always a friendly and outgoing personality, Clarice would soon form friendships with other young people from the Caribbean who, like herself, aspired to a career by attending various courses at the same college. Although she was no "flapper" or even occasional "party girl", Clarice might now and again accept an invitation to attend a house-party or get-together organised by friends. She loved fashion and always made sure that she was "dressed to impress" whenever she socialised with her girlfriends. She never held back from getting into the party spirit and willingly joined in as revellers grooved to the tempo of recordings of Southern Blues, known back then as Race Records, being played on a wind-up gramophone. The boys would be grouped together, glass in hand, as they enjoyed a drink and a chat, but would, now and again, extend a hand to a pretty girl and politely ask: "May I have this dance, please?" on hearing a favourite number.

It was at one such event that Clarice spotted a handsome young man leaning against a table, whilst supping intermittently from a glass. He stood alone and appeared oblivious to the noisy conversations around him. Clarice was immediately smitten. She had in the past been approached by young men who expressed an interest in her, but Clarice was determined to maintain focus on achieving her career goal, and any potential distraction was resisted. Even though she was now in her early twenties, Clarice had never been in a relationship with a man. But here she was, being irresistibly drawn to someone of the opposite sex and secretly wishing that he would at some stage ask her to join him in a dance. In those days, girls were not expected to make the first move and simply waited to be approached. But Clarice's dream was not realised that particular evening. Even though the young man appeared to have thrown away assumed inhibitions and had transformed himself into a party animal, dancing and chatting merrily with various girls at the gathering, he seemed not to have noticed her. Clarice could not help but feel a little deflated at the end of the evening, but remained hopeful that she would, sooner or later, see him again, and who knows what might happen? After all, the West Indian community in New York during the 1920s was small and the people clung to each other.

Clarice did indeed see the young man of interest at subsequent "get-togethers" or parties, but he continued to ignore her. Clarice was not deterred; she felt a sense of destiny with this particular individual and was somehow convinced that they would eventually come together. Clarice pondered on the reasons why she seemed unable to shift thoughts of this man from her mind. She had never before "day-dreamed" about any boy and had so far been successful in steering clear of any such distraction. It seemed that an uncontrollable force was at play and had taken over her emotions.

Clarice's predication regarding the person of interest was unexpectedly realised when she decided at a whim to visit a particular friend, whom she had not seen for a while. Clarice was greeted at the front door with a warm hug. "Long time no see," gushed the friend. The pair chatted excitedly and held each other's hand as they walked into the house. But Clarice was suddenly and unexpectedly silenced when she spotted a young man that resembled her "secret love" sitting on the sofa. Clarice's heart skipped a beat. Unbelievable! This cannot be him! But as these thoughts were whirling around in her mind, Clarice heard the high-pitched voice of her girlfriend, urging, "Meet my friend", while gently steering her towards the seated visitor.

He immediately sprung to his feet, flashed a huge smile that revealed a row of evenly matched pearly-white teeth, and firmly shook Clarice's hand. "Walter Ross," he declared.

It had been for Clarice a "heart-stopping" magical moment and her stomach summersaulted as she stuttered her response, "Clarice Radix. Pleased to meet you." Clarice's dream had suddenly and unexpectedly come true. Life could not be better. She considered herself a "lucky girl" to have been introduced to her "dream man". The saying, 'whatever is meant for you will never pass you by' may have at that moment crossed her mind.

The "spur of the moment" decision to visit her friend would evolve into an unanticipated enchanting evening. The three young friends sat comfortably in each other's company and their conversations flowed freely. Clarice would discover that Walter was also born and raised on the island of Grenada and even though they originated from different parishes, had some knowledge of each other's family background. It was at a time when nearly every person on the small Caribbean island of Grenada claimed to know or know of everyone else. Or that they were in some way related. Consequently, Clarice was not surprised and simply burst into laughter when Walter loudly and humorously exclaimed, "I hope we're not related!" Clarice was at that point blissfully happy. She could never have imagined that she had arrived at a turn in the road that would lead to her destiny.

The newly formed friendship between Clarice and Walter quickly developed into a full-blown relationship. Clarice had not previously experienced such passion. She thought of nothing and no-one but the man who had totally captivated her heart. The couple's meetings were highly anticipated and their embraces were passionately electric. Suddenly, studying was no longer the priority. Ironically, Clarice had previously avoided "love entanglements", fearing that she would be distracted from the studies that were essential for achieving her goal. But Clarice's head no longer ruled. Her heart had taken over, and she was powerless. The situation was elevated onto the next level when the couple discovered that a baby was on the way. Walter responded by pledging steadfast support. He proposed marriage and, following a small church wedding, the newly married couple set up home in Walter's rented apartment in Brooklyn, New York.

Previously, on being informed of the changed circumstances, Clarice's employers had been reluctant to let her go. They considered her a competent, reliable and trustworthy worker, but, most importantly, the children in her care "adored" her. As a consequence, the live-in contract was replaced with one in which fixed morning and evening working hours were agreed. Clarice was happy that she had been given the opportunity of continuing to earn a much-needed salary, but hoped to resume her studies after giving birth and organising a system of child-care.

Time would tell if Clarice's well-intended career plan could ever be salvaged.

All was well. Everything seemed to be running smoothly. Marriage did not cool their "hot" romance. Clarice and Walter had entered their marriage with open eyes. They pledged to support and love each other "forever" and were of the firm belief that their union would be sealed by the new arrival. Clarice had never been happier when, like a bolt out of the blue, her perfect life was shattered on receiving a telegram which stated that William, her dearly beloved father, had passed. Clarice was mortified. The unexpected devastating information significantly impacted on a smooth and free-flowing path on which no major hurdles had been anticipated.

On hearing news of her father's demise, Clarice sank into depression, made worse by feelings of regret that she was unable to make the journey to his funeral. She was at the time heavily pregnant. Walter's sustained efforts to console his wife failed. Clarice remained inconsolably tearful and desolate. William was, in her opinion, the best father ever. A gentle and caring soul who had been instrumental in ensuring that she was raised in a stable and secure family environment.

A few short months following the passing of William, Clarice gave birth to a beautiful daughter. Although both parents were delighted, Clarice was deeply saddened that her father had not lived to see his first grandchild. It seemed so unfair. He was only 49!

Despite lingering grief, Clarice managed to "step up to the plate" and succeeded in being a devoted wife and mother, while at the same time maintaining her employment commitments. But, as time went on, Clarice realised that the support she received from her husband during the initial period of their marriage was no longer being provided. Walter showed himself to be less than helpful. He expected his wife to do all the household chores such as laundry, cooking, cleaning and looking after the baby, while he relaxed in his favourite armchair. It had been a chauvinistic era and Clarice, like many other wives of the day, seemed conditioned into believing that they could do nothing but comply with wifely duties and expectations.

Only a few months after giving birth to the couple's first baby, Clarice discovered that she had again fallen pregnant. Suddenly, there were two additional children, and Clarice struggled with looking after three toddlers without "hands on" support from her husband. In those days men were not generally expected to assist with child care routines, but, with her husband's agreement, Clarice turned to her own mother, Angie, for help.

On receiving Clarice's letter requesting assistance with caring for the siblings, Angie wasted no time in replying and stating her willingness to care for the grandchildren on a full-time basis. Not only did she feel compelled to provide the young family with the help and support they needed, Angie very much looked forward to seeing Clarice again after several years of being apart. Clarice, in due course, travelled to Grenada with the siblings and placed them into the temporary care of her mother, Angie. Mother and daughter were delighted to be reunited, but it was also for Clarice an opportunity for a much-needed break.

Clarice was confident that the siblings would be safe and properly cared for by their grandmother and returned to the marital home feeling refreshed and energised. She had enjoyed an all too short vacation, but it had been filled with reconnecting with family and friends and relaxing on local beaches. Clarice was now anticipating a new start with her husband and dared to hope that the happiness shared during the early stage of their marriage could be recaptured. She embarked on a quest to repair the cracks that had appeared in their once-perfect relationship.

The rigours associated with the increasing demands placed on Clarice as she struggled single-handedly with the tasks of looking after her quickly expanding family had taken their toll. Furthermore, she had been forced to abandon her studies as it had all become too much, and her marriage suffered under the strain of it all. Despite being saddened by the deterioration in a situation that had appeared to guarantee long-lasting happiness, Clarice would become too exhausted even to care. But now, with the children in the capable hands of their grandmother, she felt that the time was right for concentrating on saving the marriage.

Clarice began her quest by paying more attention to her appearance, initiating conversation and preparing delicious meals. Walter's responses were encouraging and a certain degree of harmony returned. Two further children followed, and they also were placed in the care of their grandmother. Even though there was a marked improvement in the couple's personal interactions, Walter remained reluctant in meeting his financial responsibilities. Consequently, Clarice had no option but to find herself a second job for ensuring that the children back home were being financially supported. For Clarice, life had evolved into an un-ending hurried routine that involved rushing home from the first job and knuckling down to housekeeping tasks, before dashing off to job number two. Meanwhile, Walter appeared to be enjoying a "stress-free" life, being waited upon by a hard-pressed but tolerant wife.

After approximately seven years of marriage, Walter suggested that the couple should return to Grenada and take over the parenting of their offspring. Children needed and had the right to be raised by their biological parents, Walter asserted. Clarice did not doubt his sincerity when he put forward the idea that the couple would start up a business which should provide the necessary funds for supporting their family. Clarice was overjoyed. She could think of nothing better than being able to care for her own children, alongside their father, in a stable and loving home. Clarice felt that she was about to reap the rewards for honouring the "For Better or Worse" marriage vows by being patient and sticking with her husband during the difficult times. She was elated.

A plan to relocate was immediately put into place by the couple. It involved the purchase of a house in the homeland. Clarice would be the first to move into the new property and, after settling in with the children, Walter would follow. In the meantime, he would remain in New York, but provide the funds necessary for sustaining his family. Clarice could find no reason for doubting her husband's sincerity. It was, after all, "his idea", she assured herself.

The offspring of Clarice and Walter had been joyous to have been returned into the care of their beloved mother. Although they received excellent physical care from their grandmother Angie, her parenting style was stern and inflexible, and reinforced with the whip. Moreover, the siblings feared their "Uncle Lloyd". They would attempt to disappear from view whenever Lloyd visited, as he never failed to test their academic progress and lashed them with a "leather belt" for each error. It was, therefore, like a "breath of fresh air" to be with their mother again. She was so kind and affectionate and she would never use the dreaded whip as a method of discipline. Indeed, when "Uncle Lloyd" appeared at the family home and lifted the strap to Walter jnr after declaring that he was a "dunce" for making a spelling mistake, Clarice forcefully wrestled the belt out of her brother's hand and angrily asserted that he should never again chastise her son. And in no uncertain terms she added, "If he is a dunce, so be it. Just leave him alone!" The siblings were victorious. At last someone was prepared to step in and protect them from their caring but punitive uncle.

Many months passed by, and though Clarice had been posting weekly letters to Walter, they remained unanswered. Moreover, the promised financial assistance had not been forthcoming. Clarice was beside herself with worry and found herself in a desolate place, not knowing where to turn or who to turn to. Had Walter actually abandoned his family? Was the plan to start afresh "back home" a sham? A ploy for ridding himself of his family? Clarice was unable to silence the inner voice that nagged doubts and sought resolution to unanswered questions. The situation was at a critical point when brother Lloyd attempted to rescue things by offering to enter into and finance a furniture business venture with his sister. Clarice could not be more grateful and entered the joint enterprise with anticipation and enthusiasm.

In spite of their efforts, the business that had been set up by Clarice and Lloyd failed to show profit. It was the point at which Clarice felt that she had been backed against a wall. What should she do? She was torn between continuing the happy life she had created for her children, but with limited funds; or to consider their best interests in the long term. Clarice desired the best opportunities for her children and reasoned that she had just one option. She would return to New York and resume working two or even three jobs for ensuring they received the best educational opportunities. She was, however, distressed at the thought of having to once again separate from her children and the emotional consequences.

Clarice made a decision. She decided against disclosing to them "Mummy's" intention to return to New York.

All the while, Clarice had been harbouring disturbing gossip that Walter had found himself another woman. Although he failed to fulfil the promise of financial assistance or even maintain contact with his family, Clarice strived to remain positive. She reasoned that he was still her husband and as a consequence could, at any time, reclaim her rightful legal status. The couple would thereafter pick up on the initial plan to work towards creating a home in which they could together raise their offspring. Clarice's faith in the sanctuary of marriage and the hope of an eventual happy family existence was not diminished.

On the day of her planned departure, Clarice escorted the siblings to school and, with heavy heart, bade them goodbye with lingering hugs and kisses. She did not "look back" as she tearfully hurried from the school gates. Many years would pass before Clarice would again lay eyes on her children.

Immediately after arriving in New York, Clarice made her way to the marital home in Brooklyn and, in a hopeful frame of mind, anchored her suitcase on the ground, before firmly pressing the entry bell. A few minutes passed and an unknown woman appeared with a baby in her arms and toddler in tow. "Can I help you?" she asked politely.

"Is Walter at home"?"

"You mean my husband, Walter Ross. No, he's not home from work yet," was the unexpected reply.

Clarice was stunned. Did she actually say the words "my husband"? Clarice wondered. "Are you Walter's wife?" Clarice asked with curiosity.

"Yes, we've been married for nearly two years."

"Is that your baby?" Clarice enquired.

"Yes, we now have two little girls."

Clarice gasped as the shocking revelation impacted like a dagger through her heart. She held her breath as her head swooned and her body swayed. But Clarice was somehow able to summon her inner strength and regained her composure. "Thank you," she stuttered, as she turned and stumbled down the stairs, tears streaming down her cheeks.

The woman called out, "Do you want to leave him a message?"

"No. No," Clarice replied, and quickly disappeared from view. It had been a crushing revelation. Walter was a bigamist. He had taken a second "wife" before divorcing the first. It had been the ultimate betrayal.

Meanwhile, on the afternoon of Clarice's return to the United States, the siblings were not particularly worried that their mother was not at the school gate to collect them at the end of the school day, as was usually the case, and were instead being picked up by a family friend. But they were a little perturbed when they were dropped off at their grandmother's house. The children would soon discover that their mother had left the island and that they would be remaining in the care of their grandmother, Angie. They were shocked and shattered and spontaneously and collectively erupted into a chorus of desperate screams that resounded throughout the neighbourhood. The traumatic upheaval was long-lasting and resulted in emotional and psychological scarring and life-long psychological issues.

Always a religious woman, and strengthened by her Faith, Clarice picked herself up from the "knock down" blow. She decided against dwelling on the experience of bitter disappointment, and even blamed herself for being "naïve" and "stupid". The children were the priority, and she had to be strong for them. Clarice deeply regretted being unable to raise the siblings herself without the support of their father but vowed to do everything possible for enabling them a better future. Even though personal hopes and aspirations had been "dashed", she remained focused on doing everything possible for ensuring a better future for her children, and tirelessly juggled various jobs for making sure that the siblings "back home" received the best fee-paying education available at the time. Packages were also at regular intervals despatched and contained a variety of items including dried food, toiletries and beautiful outfits.

The years flew by and in quick succession the first four children had graduated from High School. The next step in the educational process was College attendance in the United States. Clarice secured a large apartment, before sending for her older children. The youngest child remained in the care of grandma "Nen". She had not yet reached school-leaving age and it was thought to be in her best interests that she completed her education prior to joining the family in New York. The young girl was, nonetheless, deeply unhappy to have been separated from her siblings.

The now-teenaged children were happy to be with their mother again and related well with her. Clarice was delighted to discover that they had blossomed into beautiful, intelligent and articulate young adults. It was evident that. despite being a disciplinarian, grandma "Nen" had done an excellent job in raising her charges. Eldest daughter, Beryl, recalled that her brother and sisters adjusted quickly into Clarice's care and experienced no difficulties re-establishing their relationship with her. She went on to say that Clarice had been an affectionate, caring and attentive parent, and regularly assured the siblings that they were her "golden children".

There could be no denying that Clarice made every effort to ensure that the children with whom she had been reunited were at all times comfortable and happy in her care.

Not too long after their arrival in New York, Clarice made sure that the siblings were enrolled at College and had started the process of realising their individual career aspirations. Clarice had been immensely satisfied that, even though she had been given no choice but to leave them in the care of their grandmother, they nonetheless received an excellent educational foundation, and were now on the way to an opportunistic future. Clarice was, at that juncture, a contented woman. She was heartened by the fact that the long hours that were spent working had not been undertaken in vain.

It was during this period of "plain sailing" that Clarice's second-born daughter made a startling revelation. She was pregnant. It was, for Clarice, unexpected and unwelcome news. She feared that her girl may have "thrown away" the chance of making something of herself; but, despite what may have been deemed a disappointing setback, Clarice was braced to provide her daughter with help and support as required. She had managed to overcome previous difficulties and felt certain that she would do so again. But would this be a crisis too far?

News that she was to become a grandmother had an unsettling effect on Clarice's emotional health. Past painful experiences, which were all the while being supressed, began rearing their ugly head. She had previously prided herself as being a strong woman, capable of rising above life's obstacles. She now found herself powerlessly overwhelmed by the mixture of emotions that consumed her, and she seemed to be on an emotional downward spiral. Her sparkle vanished and she became increasingly low-spirited and melancholy.

Clarice appeared less depressed following the birth of a grand-daughter. The family assumed that the new arrival had injected joy into her life and were, as a consequence, relieved. Indeed, daughter Beryl recollected that Clarice had been enamoured by her first grand-daughter and was actively involved in caring for her. The siblings were happy that their mother's mood had lifted and that she looked after the new arrival willingly, and in a loving and tender manner. It seemed that initial feelings of apprehension in relation to the birth had vanished and were replaced with joy. Consequently, it had been without warning that the family was shaken to the core by the unexpected catastrophic chain of events that were about to unfold.

Clarice suddenly snapped. The baby died in tragic circumstances and Clarice was sectioned and detained in a psychiatric facility. Clarice's husband and father of her children was notified of the crisis, but his response was disappointingly cold and non-committal. "Not my problem. I'm not her husband!" he commented with an air of dismissal. Walter conveyed little interest in the welfare of his first family. It had been, for the distressed offspring, an unbelievably shocking insight into nature of a father who appeared totally void of compassion. They were crushed.

Certified as being "insane", Clarice was for many years detained and treated in a Psychiatric Unit. She was, however, never abandoned by her family. She was visited on a regular basis by her children, and her brothers and sisters maintained an interest in her progress and well-being. And it was as a result of continuing intervention and assurances given to acting psychiatrists by her brothers that eventually secured Clarice's discharge from the facility in which she was being treated. She was released into their care and immediately thereafter returned to her country.

Having been for a while insistent that she had been cured of her condition, Clarice was now joyously liberated to have been given a second chance. However, the fact that every attempt in reconciling with her children on a permanent basis had been in one way or the other sabotaged remained an open sore in Clarice's heart. But life must go on and Clarice would embrace this new chapter with enthusiasm.

Following her arrival on home ground, Clarice spent a few weeks under the roof of one or other sibling, before moving into a family-owned house and looking for something meaningful to do. Clarice needed to have a sense of purpose, and when she discovered that her elderly Aunt Evie was not being properly cared for at the Residential Home in which she had been placed, Clarice became concerned, and her caring and nurturing spirit kicked in. She made the decision to take matters into her own hands by moving Evie, who had been suffering from dementia, into her home. Clarice would deliver the best possible overall care and attention to her ailing aunt until the end of her life. Ironically, it had been a case of life coming full circle. Clarice's mother, Angie, had been her youngest sister Evie's main substitute carer during the first years of her life.

Clarice's desire to realise her unfulfilled care-giving needs did not end with the demise of Aunt Evie. She would, along the way, reach out by fostering children whose parents may have required assistance or support. In spite of her altruistic endeavours, Clarice never lost her entrepreneur spirit. She was a highly motivated visionary who independently set up and ran two successful retail businesses.

Although she could on occasions appear irritated, or some may say "highly strung", overall, Clarice had been considered a "giving" and religious individual who had never been heard to utter a "bad word" about anyone. Even when asked about her feelings regarding the husband who betrayed her, Clarice refused to wallow in self-pity or be drawn into negative thinking and focused only on happier times. "At least I married the man I loved," she said, while flashing the brightest of smiles.

After experiencing an idyllic early life, Clarice expected that a bright future would be hers for the taking, provided she worked for it. She was prepared to apply herself and do everything required for realising her dreams. But it was not to be. By a quirk of fate, she found herself being de-railed from what appeared to be a predictably marked-out path, and onto a hard road on which there were many obstacles. She would not, however, be bowed, and somehow found the strength to keep going for the sake of her children. Their future success became the priority on which she focused.

Despite having to endure a life plagued by bitter disappointments, painful separations, betrayal and hard work, Clarice remained strong in spirit and strengthened in faith, and was, in the end, rewarded for her sacrifices. She was triumphant that each of her five children had found personal happiness, fulfilling and successful careers, were happy and enjoyed comfortable lifestyles. The aspirations she desired for herself had been finally achieved through her children.

Clarice spent her last days in quiet contentment at a Nursing Home and died peacefully in her sleep at the age of 83.

Clarice Radix
1903 - 1986

BEST THINGS IN LIFE ARE FREE

Ivan was the first of Angie and William's twelve surviving children. He was, to the then seventeen-year-old mother, a fragile and delicate bundle of joy, and the infant was mollycoddled from day one. As a growing boy, Ivan had been susceptible to infection. He was, as a consequence, treated with special care and attention, but some would say that he had been "wrapped in cotton wool" by his doting and obsessive young mother.

As with his younger brothers and sisters, Ivan had been required to attend school on a daily basis. But even though he showed little interest in his school work, unlike the other siblings, Ivan was never pressured by his parents into doing better. He was instead encouraged to pursue his interests in sport, having been athletic and particularly gifted in a variety of sporting activities. Moreover, Ivan was spared from being harshly disciplined within a household where children were expected to be seen but not heard, and the whip ruled. Despite this fact, he remained unspoilt and maintained a humorous, playful and protective relationship with his siblings. They in turn loved and respected their big brother and in no way resented his bestowed "princely" status.

Although Ivan had not been particularly interested in academia, he was nevertheless fundamentally intelligent. But Angie and William had been pleasantly surprised and very proud that he had actually stepped up to the plate when it was required, and passed his school-leaving examinations with distinction. Unlike his brothers and other young people of the day, Ivan had no inclination of venturing too far beyond the borders of his community. He resisted being seduced by stories of the progressive and opportunistic lifestyles that lay beyond the island's shores and was not even interested in visiting the city of St. George. Ivan loved the rural surroundings into which he had been born and was comfortable. As far as he was concerned, there was no place better, and remained single-minded in his decision to "stay put". Needless to say, Angie was delighted that the son with whom she was obsessed would never be far away from home.

Ivan did, however, have a plan for earning his livelihood and sustaining his chosen lifestyle, and was reassured that both parents expressed encouragement and pledged to provide the required assistance and support when he revealed to them his ambition to open up and manage his own grocery store. Before too long, a small house with adjoining adequate space for operating a shop was being made available to the young man with initiative. Even so, Ivan would continue to live at home while focusing on building up his little business on a day-to-day basis. Angie could not be happier that her favourite son remained a member of the household and secretly wished that he would never leave her side. There were, at that point, no clues that the adored Ivan had all the while been anticipating taking the bold step of venturing out on his own and that a surprise announcement was imminent.

Angie could have been "knocked down by a feather" when Ivan brought home an attractive young lady and announced his intention of asking for her hand in marriage. Both William and Angie were stunned and speechless. Neither had any idea that Ivan may have been in a personal relationship, let alone thinking of getting married! Without warning, the couple found themselves being jolted into reality. The seemingly vulnerable "mother's boy" had been all the while operating in the manner of a "very dark horse". But, unbeknown to the family, Ivan had reached a point when he believed that he should take control of his life by laying down roots for the future. On coming to terms with the "bombshell" revelation, Angie and William congratulated the young couple and went on to express their approval that Ivan had chosen a "nice girl" to be his future wife. In a locality where everyone knew, or knew of, everyone else, both parents were aware that this particular young lady lived in a nearby village and came from a "good family".

The in-laws-to-be could not be more pleased that Ivan had chosen their daughter to be his future wife. "The boy has good prospects," they said, and willingly consented to the marriage. Within a relatively short time, the two families had come together and a wedding was being planned. It would be a small church ceremony, followed by a jolly reception with food and drink in abundance. After the celebrations, Ivan and his bride moved into the house that had been provided by William and settled into married life. The daily routines involved Ivan opening up the shop immediately following a substantial breakfast prepared by a dutiful wife, who was subsequently kept busy by the various housekeeping chores.

Although Angie was pleased that Ivan had found his "soul mate", she was at the same time downhearted that she may no longer be first in his affections. Essentially, she did not want her "little boy" to grow up, nor was she prepared to surrender her control over him. And on various occasions she appeared at the home Ivan shared with his wife, set the scene for an argument and affirmed her power by slapping her married son sharply across the face in the presence of his wife! Angie knew well that the young couple were at all times respectful of their elders and would never even dream of retaliating. But she never failed being the loving and attentive parent whenever Ivan visited the family home. He was, on those treasured occasions, once again her baby, and she interacted with him in soft and tender tones. In response, Ivan would take on a child-like role and reply in corresponding infantile vocabulary.

Ivan appeared unable to break away from his mother's steadfast grip, but there was no denying that the pair shared an unbreakable emotional and psychological attachment.

Despite this fact, Ivan was committed to his marriage and made every effort to be a good husband. He loved his wife and hoped that his marriage would be as successful as his parents'. The young couple were not, however, destined to have a family. At a time when large families had been the accepted norm, they were the exception. After many childless years, Ivan and his wife had given up all hope of producing an offspring, when, out of the blue, "Miss Ivan" discovered that she was expecting. The couple were ecstatic at the prospect of being first-time parents and prepared, with joyous anticipation, for the new arrival. But they would be struck a crushing blow. The infant daughter died shortly after birth.

Ivan and his wife clung to each other for comfort as they jointly grieved their crippling loss. They would, in time, learn to live without their beloved daughter, but she was not forgotten. Their hope of conceiving for a second time remained undiminished as the years flew by. Ivan's retail business flourished; he became the most popular shopkeeper in his community of the era and was affectionately known as "Cousin Ivan". Always a generous and considerate individual, Ivan had been aware of the poverty endured by various families who resided in the locality. Consequently, goods on credit were reliably available, but he was also willing to accept nutmegs or even cocoa as payment for items purchased. Ivan enjoyed the company of children and hungry youngsters were free to congregate in his shop after school, and handfuls of broken crackers accompanied by lumps of cheese would be distributed among them. Essentially an easy-going, jolly character with a chuckle in his voice, Ivan spent his days not only serving customers but conversing and cracking jokes with them. He was indeed a happy and contented soul who could think of no better occupation. Ivan was never influenced or even impressed by his younger brothers' professional successes and material possessions. And while they drove big cars, he was quite happy getting around on horseback.

Ivan loved the peace and tranquillity of the countryside. He felt at one with the surrounding nature and the natural sounds produced by the elements, accompanied by singing birds, buzzing insects and animal cries had been music to his ears. Ivan and his wife kept a variety of domestic and farm animals and invitees to lunch may be led to the chicken coop filled with colourful birds and asked to select their preference for stewing. But visitors to the house were often enchanted by the sweet aroma that wafted from trays of nutmeg, mace and cocoa that had been laid out to "dry" at the front door.

Despite the lingering ache associated with the loss of their child and a continued unfulfilled wish for a family, the couple's love for each other remained strong and they were happy. Indeed, life was going swimmingly and seemed forever when "Miss Ivan" was unexpectedly taken, following a brief illness. It seemed to Ivan that a rug had been pulled from under his feet and he struggled. There was, however, no shortage of help from sympathetic unattached females who flocked to his side. Although the local shop-keeper had been considered a "good catch", women had been attracted to his good looks and friendly and approachable demeanour. Moreover, Ivan seemed to bring out their maternal instinct. Like his mother, Angie, they all wanted to look after him, and he enjoyed being mothered.

One of Ivan's female admirers was Doris Francis, a gentle, soft-spoken school teacher from a respected family. Ivan took a shine to this particular woman's warm and caring persona and the couple became an item. But Angie was not too pleased and made clear her disapproval when, within months of the devastating loss, Ivan insisted on being married for the second time. Despite his grief, Ivan, who had never previously lived by himself, felt unable to cope without the supportive and comforting presence of a live-in partner. He would, therefore, ignore his mother's objections and take a new wife.

The years marched on, but expectations that children would be produced from the union were not realised. However, on hearing word of a partially sighted little girl with learning difficulties who had been abandoned by her mother, the couple decided to welcome the child into their home. In an age when the majority of children slept on the floor in a communal space, this particular child was privileged with a room of her own, complete with single bed. She also received very good care by two people who were committed to meeting her needs. A gentle soul who was always eager to please, the little girl presented no challenges to her substitute parents. The family were happy and Ivan, in particular, discovered a new sense of purpose from being a father at long last. But it would all be taken away much too soon. The delightful daughter passed away when she was still only a teenager. She was sadly mourned by her parents and those who knew and loved her.

Life in the marital home was pleasant and calm, but the couple regularly entertained friends and relatives including members of the Lett family who lived lived in the parish of St David. Ivan was particularly joyful when his young nieces and nephews came to stay and would entertain them with hilarious tales of his boyhood experiences. Meanwhile, Ivan maintained his regular routine, which involved opening up shop every morning. There were always a few children waiting at the shop-door to deliver a message to "Cousin Ivan" from their mother. The message was usually: "Please send half-pound of sugar, a can of condensed milk, a few sticks of matches or even a few grains of salt, for making breakfast for the children before school. Will bring some nutmeg later or pay you at the end of the month." Of course, "Cousin Ivan" understood the needs of his poverty-stricken neighbours and was at all times agreeable to their requests.

Ivan had not been at all times robustly healthy. He was throughout his life asthmatic and susceptible to chest infections and sought to protect himself by always wearing a flannel vest underneath his shirt. However, when he found that he was unable to "pee", Ivan told no-one. He may have been unaware of the serious implications of the problem, but decided to tell no-one and believed that it would eventually right itself. It was not to be. Overcome by excruciating pain, Ivan sought consultation with his brother, Dr John, and as a result was immediately rushed to the General Hospital, located in the city of St George, for an emergency procedure. It was destined to be his first and last journey away from his beloved rural community. He would succumb from "renal failure" at just 57 years of age.

Ivan's untimely passing in his middle years had been a devastating loss not only for his loved ones, but also for the local community. Many tears were shed.

Ivan lived a quiet and simple life. He held no interest or curiosity of life in the wider, more progressive world. He did not possess a vast amount of money, live in a large house, own a car or harbour any desire for material wealth. Moreover, his humble dwelling contained no electricity or running water. His only transport had been a reliable old horse he called "Ben". Ivan chose the simple life and, by so doing, was happily stress-free and content. Moreover, he never experienced life without an adoring woman by his side who willingly met his every need. He was enriched by love.

Ivan Radix
1902 - 1958

LONE STAR

Always a loner, Matthias, commonly known as Tokes had been the sixth offspring produced by William and Angie Radix. Tox was, during his childhood years, somewhat detached from his siblings. He was quiet, thoughtful and appeared to be in a world of his own. Unlike his brother O'Hanley before him, Tokes was not a particularly problematic child. Even so, he was never spared being whipped by his mother for the smallest indiscretion, but craved recognition for the things he did well. In a ploy for receiving positive attention, Tokes stole his mother's purse and subsequently offered to help in the frantic search when she realised it had vanished. Angie screamed with delight when the "devious son" suddenly exclaimed: "I found it! I found it!" She was relieved and, in a show of gratitude, spontaneously threw her arms around the emotionally needy child. The memorable moment would never recur. It was the one and only "hug" Tokes recalled ever receiving from his mother as a growing boy. He was, however, throughout his childhood, very much valued by his father, William. He was also secure in his sense of belonging and being an inclusive member of the tightly knit family fold.

Although he had very few friends at school, Tokes had been considered an exemplary pupil by his teachers, and both Angie and William were happy but not surprised that he had received high grades in his school-leaving examinations. Following the death of his beloved father, Tokes expressed to his mother the desire to seek employment in South America. Angie accepted the fact that her now-grown son needed to find his own way in life and, along with her blessings, provided him with the required financial assistance. departed with the promise that he would write to his family after arriving on foreign soil. But Angie was sorely disappointed when the expected letter failed to appear. made no contact with his family following his departure. As a consequence, no-one knew his whereabouts or whether he was dead or alive.

Angie would worry about her errant son and pray daily for his safety and welfare throughout her remaining years.

The family were dumbfounded when, after a long period of absence, Tokes unexpectedly reappeared. Suddenly, long-held concerns relating to his well-being were being replaced with relief and joy that Tokes was alive and well, and he was welcomed with open arms. But Tokes' happiness on returning home turned into sorrow on being told that Angie was no longer among them. He regretted not keeping the promise of maintaining contact with her and was overcome with feelings of guilt. But Tokes was reassured by the fact that family bonds remained intact and that their love and support were reliably consistent.

After twenty years of living and working abroad, Tokes was pleased to discover that the island had been catching up with the modern world. It was now the 1950s. A period when there were a documented 1,903 licensed vehicles on the road. The figures included buses that transported individuals into the city for work or school on a regular daily basis. There was an increased number of retail businesses, social clubs and eateries. Cinemas featured not only the latest movies, but also internal news. It had been Tokes' overall view that the slow-paced ancient town of long ago had been transformed into a relatively progressive little city.

Always a private individual, Tokes did not disclose to others his occupation during the period he spent in South America. It was, however, generally assumed that, after many years of employment, he should have accumulated sufficient funds for being self-reliant. Tokes stayed at the home of various "better off" family members, before stating his intention to relocate permanently to the then unoccupied house in which he was raised, in the village of Vincennes, St David's. Despite the relatively enlightened lifestyle of the city, Tokes had decided that he had had enough of the bright lights, having for many years lived and worked in Venezuela. Moreover, Tokes was essentially a loner. He enjoyed his own company and being free to be himself.

The house in which Tokes and his siblings were brought up had been unlived-in for a considerable period. Despite this fact, Tokes was certain that the once homely atmosphere would be re-generated by his presence. Entering the building brought back bitter/sweet memories of how it used to be. Tox was, however, not deterred and maintained the determination to make the abandoned building his home. After deciding upon and organising his living quarters, Tokes quickly settled into a single but peacefully pleasant existence in the old house. He would often sit and cast his mind on a bygone era and laugh out aloud while recalling specific memorable moments. They had been, for him, the good old days. Thoughts of unpleasant occurrences had without doubt been side-stepped during those starry-eyed journeys down memory lane.

Although he had been away from the area for a considerable period, Tokes experienced no difficulty readjusting to country life. He wasted no time renewing links with old acquaintances and family members who continued to reside in the locality. But he was always welcomed at the homes of siblings Daniel and Ivan, who lived in a nearby village, and the jovial threesome often reminisced on past times.

Tokes was described as being pleasantly reserved, well-spoken, and a proper "gentleman" by all who knew him. He was also a humorous character and a hilarious tale was always at the tip of his tongue. Many recalled the stories about his adventures in Venuzuela. Local children would be awestruck as they listened intently to his detailed accounts of the wild animals he encountered, and wrestled with, including "giant snakes"! No-one knew for sure whether the bizarre daring and hazardous escapades had been fact or fiction. But it could not be denied that Tokes had been a captivating and illustrative storyteller.

Essentially a reclusive soul who always walked alone, Tokes would naturally withdraw back into himself following moments of interactions with others. He never married and remained a deeply private person. No-one knew for sure whether or not he had ever been in a long-term relationship or fathered children. It was generally accepted that Tokes had been, without doubt, content in his chosen lifestyle, but he was also aware of the unwavering support that was always forthcoming from his brothers and sisters. They were his anchor. Consequently, when he eventually ran out of money, Tokes periodically called on his "well-to-do" brothers who lived in the city and offered to undertake various tasks in return for cash. Even though they understood his plight and had been willing, unconditionally, to provide him with the necessary funds, Tokes, who was fundamentally a decent and proud individual, refused to accept hand-outs.

The family, as well as those in the community in which he lived, were aware that Tokes had a problem with alcohol. He was never seen without a bottle of rum in his back pocket and it was suspected that all his money went on drink, although he never appeared unkempt or to be under the influence of alcohol. Nonetheless, rum had been his comforting constant companion. He loved nothing better than cosying-up with his bottle and drinking himself to sleep at night.

In spite of his "addiction", Tokes' lifestyle was not chaotic. He maintained a regular schedule, and fishing and working the field had been integral to his daily routines. He spent much of his time tending family-owned land and planting crops. Tokes snacked on reaped seasonal produce such as fruit and nuts. Vegetables, including the root variety, would often be steamed and, with the "catch of the day", consumed with relish, and washed down with large gulps of liquor, straight from the bottle.

Tragedy struck unexpectedly while Tokes had been carrying out an everyday function. He climbed a tree with the intention of picking a particular vegetable to be prepared for luncheon when he lost his footing and fell, after mistakenly grabbing hold of a weakened branch. Tokes did not survive the fall. He had unfortunately broken his neck. He was reported to have been under the influence of alcohol at the time of the accident. News of the unbelievably horrifying misadventure reverberated across the community and beyond. The family were deeply shocked that their harmless brother, uncle, nephew and cousin had been so cruelly taken at the relatively young age of 50.

A solitary individual from childhood, Tokes lived alone, ate alone and walked a lonesome road. He did not share his thoughts but appeared satisfied with the life he lived. He never complained or expected to be provided with a free lunch from anyone. Tokes remained self-reliant throughout his days. Always respected, he is remembered kindly and with affection by surviving family members and those who knew him best.

Mathias "Tokes"
Radix
1909 - 1959

ESSENTIALLY GRASSROOTS

Daniel was an outgoing and gregarious individual who, throughout his life, had been at heart a country boy who strived to help the disadvantaged within his community. Daniel also loved entertaining and making others happy. There was always plenty of food, drink and music at his periodically organised parties. The high point for the host was the satisfaction gained from stepping back and surveying, with pleasure, guests having a good time. Daniel regularly hired men to assist with working his lands and may, at a whim, invite them all to his house for lunch. On such occasions, he would observe the ravenous workers tuck into the home-cooked meal and exclaim with delight: "I can see all you really enjoying the food!"

The ninth son born to William and Angie Radix, Daniel, like the rest of his siblings, had been tightly reined. Daily school attendance was compulsory, but they were not permitted to linger on the streets at the end of the school day. If the youngsters did not arrive home at the set time, they would be severely punished with the dreaded whip. But Daniel was no less an adventurous spirit: he loved the outdoors, and on particular days when the siblings were allowed free periods out of the house, Daniel would be drawn to the company of other boys. He was an active participator in their free-spirited and energetic jaunts, boisterous escapades, curious explorations, and hilarious conversations. Boys, in Daniel's view, were challenging, competitive and vibrant creatures, unlike girls, whom he felt were dull and boring. As a growing boy and young adolescent, Daniel harboured a passionate dislike for young females in the locality and very much resented the interest they showed in him. He ignored the fact that they may have been pretty and simply considered them "nuisances". He wished, passionately, that they would all just go away and leave him alone!

Daniel achieved well in school and received excellent grades, particularly in English Language and English Grammar, in his end-of-school examinations. But even though he was considered a gifted writer whose short stories had been published in various journals of the period, Daniel decided to take up an apprenticeship in agriculture, a popular career choice for school-leavers of his generation who hailed from rural areas.

Daniel's initial steps into young adulthood coincided with what may have appeared an overnight "conversion" into the religion of women, when sexual hormones unexpectedly came into play. He suddenly found himself being bewitched by the previously despised species and was soon exploiting his charm and good looks for scoring girlfriends. Furthermore, he was, at the time, the only boy in the district to have owned a motorcycle and, as a consequence, may have been viewed as somewhat of a "celebrity". Riding at speed was undoubtedly an exciting buzz. The noisy two-wheeler could be heard from a distance before it was seen zooming by at various points up and down the island, and Daniel was often confronted by small groups of giggly, excited girls, vying for his attention. The privileged few that were invited to accompany their "idol" on rides were subsequently often faced with hostility from envious contemporaries. It was, for Daniel, an unforgettable period filled with youthful exuberance and plenty of girlfriends.

Daniel was just nine years old when he lost his father William. He was, as a consequence, raised by his single-parent mother, Angie, for the majority of his childhood. Despite being a stern disciplinarian, Angie did not overlook the fact that Daniel had been a helpful boy. When the family had fallen on hard times following the demise of the main breadwinner, Daniel willingly participated in combined efforts as everyone pulled together to keep the family's head above water. Consequently, when he expressed his ambition to become an Ophthalmic Optician, Angie did not hesitate in giving him her full support. Daniel admired the professional successes of his older brothers. He was proud of them but felt that he was also intellectually equipped for being a high achiever.

As with his brothers before him, Daniel was offered a place to study Ophthalmology at a university in Washington DC, after obtaining a pass in the required entry examination. Angie was proud of her ambitious son and wished him success. "Arr go pray for yuh," she said, before tearfully bidding him goodbye on his departure.

Despite receiving financial assistance from specific family members, Daniel supported himself by working at a hotel carrying guests' luggage to and from parked buses or waiting taxis during free periods. But he remained focused on his studies and, at the end of the required period of training, graduated with flying colours. After returning home, Daniel set up an Ophthalmic Practice in the city of St George. It had been quite an accomplishment to have realised his long-held career goal.

There was, initially, no uncertainty in Daniel's mind regarding his chosen profession and the fulfilment that would be derived from providing a valuable service. It was a stage at which Daniel could not have imagined being steered onto an alternative path. Nonetheless, as time went by, he became increasingly bored with the slow-paced day-to-day operations of the Practice and reflected on his previous lifestyle and active involvement in the local community. Feelings of doubt and dis-satisfaction intensified and the day arrived when Daniel felt compelled to accept that he was first and foremost a people person. He would, then and there, make a career-changing decision. Daniel abandoned his Practice and followed the calling to serve his people.

The GULP (Grenada United Labour Party) was founded by Eric Gairy in 1951. Gairy advocated Rights for the poorest in the society of the period and his campaign had been initiated with an organised national strike. Over 6,500 under-paid manual workers throughout the land responded to the call. It would signal an historical awakening as the previously down-trodden marchers, emboldened by their leader, Eric Gairy, collectively demanded their right to a living wage. They were no longer prepared to be exploited by the economically privileged. It had been the first time a Political Leader spoke for the largely ignored lower classes, and they were buoyed into recognising their worth. Gairy was on a serious mission to raise standards. The people loved him and he became affectionately known as "Uncle Gairy". It was, therefore, not unexpected that the GULP headed by Eric Gairy won six of the eight contested seats at the tri-island state's first General Election held in October 1951.

Always a man of the people, Daniel had been fiercely supportive of Gairy and his humanitarian policies. He followed Gairy's progress with interest and was influenced into embarking on a new and more worthwhile career path by becoming a member of the popular GULP. He would go on to represent the Party in the constituency of St David's in the General Elections of 1954. Daniel called himself "the darling hero" as he reached out to his constituents, and compellingly delivered the altruistic policies of his Party. He received assistance from his brothers during a campaign that reached every corner within the Parish of St David. And trucks with campaigners on loudspeakers cruised through the streets, urging the people to place their vote for "the darling hero" throughout the day of the election.

There was an overall sense of relief when voting was eventually closed on election day. But even though the hard work was over, it was now being replaced by anxiety. Would the desired outcome be achieved? An atmosphere of tension prevailed as Daniel and his supporters waited nervously while the votes were being counted. After what was felt to be an eternity, the parties' representatives were summoned to appear for the results. They stood patiently and responded with respectful clapping as the various results were announced. After an agonising wait, Daniel Radix, representative of the GULP in the Parish of St David, was confirmed to have received the majority votes and declared "Winner". The announcement was followed by an eruption of jubilant cheering and congratulatory hugs and handshakes. The momentous victory was celebrated with impromptu street parties and joyous gatherings that would continue throughout the night.

Daniel was committed in his role as a newly elected member of Parliament in the Lower House of Representatives and he became a well-liked and respected "man of the people". There was no denying that he was on the correct career path, and he endeavoured to use his platform for bringing about improvements within his constituency.

In his personal life and prior to embarking on a professional career, Daniel's interest in women was not diminished, and his various affairs had resulted in a few unplanned pregnancies. This was not an uncommon occurrence in an era when contraception was largely unavailable, and babies were generally welcomed as little blessings from God. But these children had been fully acknowledged and carried their father's surname. Daniel would, however, eventually decide to settle down. The life-changing decision came at a stage in his life when he realised that he was getting older and should therefore put an end to his reckless womanising and lay down some roots. He went on to marry a respected local school teacher who was commonly known in the community in which they lived as "Teacher Lenny". The couple produced three sons together and adopted a little girl.

Son Darnley said that the disciplining of the children had been the responsibility of their mother, but she was, nonetheless, caring and nurturing, and well-loved by her husband and children. Daniel was described as being an affectionate, generous and fun-loving parent, always jovial, full of life and enjoyed telling jokes. He applied no pressure in relation to the siblings' performance at school, but achievements, whether large or small, were highly praised. Daniel loved domestic as well as farm animals, and the boys were required to assist with looking after the various species, which included dogs, cats, rabbits, pigs, goats and chickens. They were also expected to work the land alongside their father, but in due course were enthused to be permitted to share their father's interests and skills in all things mechanical.

In parallel with his family commitments, motor vehicles and driving at speed had been Daniel's personal passions. He was stimulated by the thrill of the risk and progressed from speeding motor-cycles in his youth to being at the wheel of fast-driven cars when he became an adult. Indeed, younger sibling Eileen recalled an incident when she had been a front-seat passenger in a vehicle driven by her brother, Daniel. He allegedly accelerated on approaching a sharp corner. The reckless action resulted in the passenger door suddenly flying open and Eileen being abruptly thrown out of the vehicle. Daniel continued onwards for a few minutes but, on realising what had happened, he reversed, hauled the stunned and bedraggled young woman back into the car and proceeded to blame her for causing the accident. "You should have been holding on tight!" he scolded.

Daniel's tenure as a Member of Parliament covered a period when a climate of upliftment prevailed. Importantly, the lower classes were confident that their best interests were being served by a Political Party that cared about their welfare. They were, however, encouraged to help themselves by being allocated plots of land on which crops could be cultivated. It had been a time of progression for those who struggled. In spite of these positive factors, the people's hero, Eric Gairy, was, in 1957, disenfranchised for five years. But the subsequently held General Election contested by GULP (Grenada United Labour Party), GNP (Grenada General Party) and the PDM (People's Democratic Movement) produced no clear winner.

In the absence of Gairy as leader of the GULP, Daniel decided to run as an Independent Candidate under the title "The Darling Hero" at the 1961 Elections. His brothers and various other close family members and friends supported a campaign that incorporated public meetings and street parties. The responses appeared favourable and those involved were hopeful of a good outcome. Consequently, when voting was closed on election day, Daniel and his supporters waited with optimistic bated breath as the votes were being counted. But expectations were dashed and replaced by bitter disappointment when it was determined that "The Darling Hero" had lost by a considerable margin to the GULP, the Party Daniel had abandoned in favour of running as an independent. It had been a stark realisation that even though the leader of GULP had been disenfranchised, the people remained loyal to the man they considered their saviour, "Uncle Gairy", by voting in the Political Party he founded.

Although he never lost interest in the welfare of the people, Daniel did not again enter Politics. He returned to agriculture, which had been his first occupation of choice, and provided employment to a number of individuals by hiring landworkers on a seasonal basis. He also helped the young with securing jobs outside of the community. Meanwhile, Daniel maintained a contract position in the United States, where he provided a service for several months each year. Daniel would reliably return from his working trips abroad bearing gifts, not only for his immediate family, but also the have-nots who lived locally.

Despite the work commitment that resulted in long periods of separation on an annual basis, and the fact that it had been an open secret that he had on occasions strayed from his marriage, Daniel's relationship with his wife remained strong. And the couple became closer as the children grew up and in turn flew the nest. On the day he complained of feeling unwell, the doctor was immediately called, but he would lose consciousness in the arms of his wife prior to the arrival of the medic. Daniel had been taken suddenly and unexpectedly from a heart attack. Family and friends were devastated and the community as a whole were shocked on hearing the sad news of the well-known figure who had been seen out and about just minutes prior to his demise.

Daniel is being remembered warmly and with humour by family and friends, and also the community in which he lived. He was not just a charismatic personality, he was also a well-intentioned contributor. An individual possessed of great heart who made his mark by being a man of the people. His legacy lives on.

Daniel Radix
1915 - 1986

SEIZE THE MOMENT

Thomas was the baby of the family and the last of nine surviving brothers. He was, as a consequence, ignored by the older boys or bullied by those who were nearer his age. After the birth of their youngest sister, Eileen, the siblings had been convinced that their family was complete. Consequently, when a baby boy appeared two years later, it seems that he may have been thought of as an unwelcome intruder into their already tight sibling circle and his presence was resented. The "persecutors" could not, however, break the little man's spirit or his inherent sense of worth, and Thomas remained resilient. He refused to be intimidated into settling for being the "poor relation" and made sure he received his entitled share of what he felt was important, including whatever treats that were being distributed. And he was certainly not afraid to demand large servings at meal times. Despite being assertive in ensuring his "Rights", Thomas remained powerless in deterring his brothers from the abuse they inflicted on him. He was, however, often comforted by his compassionate older sister, Rosie, and younger sibling, Eileen, had been a loyal ally and playmate. The pair shared a love of fishing and spent much of their leisure periods "catching" crayfish in a nearby river.

Thomas was just five years old when he lost his father. William had returned home subsequent to falling sick while working abroad, but he did not recover from his mystery illness. Thoughts of the kind and demonstratively affectionate man whose presence seemed all too brief were forever ingrained into Thomas' memory. He bemoaned the absence of his father throughout his childhood years and, in particular, when he was being victimised by his brothers. Thomas felt certain that William would have protected him by demanding an end to the ceaseless bullying. On the contrary, he feared his mother. Even though Thomas received excellent physical care and had been enrolled as a Boy Scout, alongside his brothers, Angie was no less a stern matriarch. The whip was at all times readily available for use by a mother who was perceived as being unsympathetic and unapproachable.

Although he formed very few friendships at the school house he attended, Thomas was smart and excelled in his school work. After leaving school, he applied successfully to become a Teacher. In those days, competent school leavers were often selected to pass on the education curriculum to continuing pupils. Following the outbreak of war in 1939, Thomas, aged 18, had been among large numbers of young men across the Caribbean who applied to join up with the Allied Forces. Thomas was accepted into the British Merchant Navy. Angie was proud of her son's courageous initiative, but feared for his safety. Thomas, on the other hand, had been realistic in his assessment of the potential risks and was prepared to "die" for the greater good.

Thomas was posted onto a British Military Ship, but his main duties would be carried out below deck.

When war ended in May 1945, Thomas' ship had been on patrol in Caribbean waters, but on the return journey to the UK it docked for refuelling at New York harbour. It was at this point that Thomas decided to grab his chance for a better future. He had heard about the American Dream. Indeed, his older brothers had achieved highly in this land of opportunity. Never one to pass over an opportunity or shy away from ensuring his "Rights", Thomas felt that he had every right to seize the opportunistic moment with which he was being presented.

And so it was that Thomas vanished into thin air. Those who waited in vain, and subsequently wondered why he had not returned to his ship, could not have known that Thomas was far gone. He had boarded a Greyhound bus and was headed for Washington DC. Thereafter, he would settle in a locality called Maryland and be taken on as a "Bellboy" at a large hotel. "Bellboys" were employees responsible for carrying luggage to and from parked vehicles.

Before too long, Thomas had started the process of eventually achieving his career goal. He applied to sit the examination for entry into the Howard University Medical School and was over the moon on receiving written confirmation that he had successfully met the academic requirements and, as a result, was being accepted for medical training. Thomas switched to permanently working the night shift and much of his salary was accumulated for paying the required fees. His days were often split between attending classes and studying in his tiny apartment.

Everything appeared to be going to plan and Thomas considered himself fortunate that he had embarked on the road to realising his dream occupation. The risk he had taken by becoming an illegal immigrant and being largely invisible amongst the multitude was, in his mind, "well worth it". But Thomas would one day discover that the complacency that was generated by the initial lucky breaks would evaporate into reality when he was, out of the blue, alerted by one of his tutors that the Authorities had approached the university regarding his residence status. Thomas was instantly alarmed and wasted no time in his response. He quickly gathered his few belongings together, hopped on a Greyhound bus and stayed put until it arrived at its final destination, which happened to be Chicago.

Thomas was captivated by the sights and sounds of the vibrant city and it seemed an appropriate place for starting afresh. But, mindful that the Authorities had been aware of his illegal entry into the United States, he decided to change his name. He was, from then on, officially known as Frank Hayling, and it was under the newly acquired identity that he was again employed as a Bellboy. Despite being bitterly disappointed and regretful that he had failed to accomplish his professional ambition, he may have concluded that "it was not to be". But returning to the homeland was not an option that Frank was at that point prepared to consider. He decided to carry on with the rest of his life in the land of opportunity and choice and felt sure that he would eventually think of an alternative worthwhile career.

It was while he was working as a Bellboy in Chicago that Frank became acquainted with the resident pianist, an African-American woman who, on a nightly basis, entertained guests with her driving renditions of the various music genres of the day. These included Be-Bop, Swing, Boogie-Woogie and Rhythm & Blues. Frank loved the exciting sounds of the late 1940s and would tap his feet while observing the musician's performances from the side-lines, during breaks from his busy schedule.

The initial platonic friendship between "Frank" and his favourite pianist gradually developed into a full-blown relationship. Apart from their similar interest in music, the pair discovered that they also shared a liking for alcohol, and much of their leisure times together would be spent socialising in bars and clubs. Frank never failed to be amazed by how his large but nimble-footed girlfriend maintained effortless fluidity as they danced the fast-moving jive. He would spin her around but, without missing a beat, she immediately picked up on the furious backward and forward stepping and was ready for yet another rhythmically timed spin. "You are better than me!" Frank exclaimed loudly, as he beamed with pleasure at the height of the jollifications.

Frank had been totally enamoured by his lady and after a relatively short period of time decided to take their relationship to the next level. He felt that they were compatible, had plenty in common, enjoyed spending time together; but, most importantly, Frank was comfortable in her company. He considered himself a lucky man; but, moreover, was certain that an opportunity had presented itself, and he intended to grab it with both hands. Frank proposed to his love interest and she was delighted. He could not be happier. Not only would this talented American musician, whom he loved dearly, become his wife, but outstanding issues relating to his illegal status in the country would be once and for all resolved. Bullseye!

Following the small wedding ceremony, "Frank" moved into the home of the new Mrs Hayling and the pair settled happily into married life. They would nonetheless encounter raised eyebrows when seen out and about together due to their contrasting stature. Frank, who was slightly built, appeared minute alongside his tall, strapping and buxom wife, and the pair were humorously titled "little and large". The couple was not, however, perturbed by the snide remarks. They loved each other, were happy and were unconcerned about the opinions of others. In due course, the couple's happiness was cemented by the arrival of a beautiful baby boy. It was a stage in the marital relationship when it seemed that the good life would just keep rolling on.

Frank and his wife looked forward to creating a happy family life with their new baby; but, as with the majority of marriages, there were, over time, difficulties to overcome. In this particular case, a shared love of alcohol that previously aroused pleasurable emotions evolved into triggering angry outbursts, allegedly instigated by a spouse who had been increasingly demanding of her husband. In reverse, Frank's naturally subdued and mild-mannered character remained unchanged. He endeavoured to keep the peace by refusing to engage in heated arguments. He would simply back down, rightfully or wrongfully accept the blame and be apologetic.

In reality, the novelty of the romance was no more and, apart from their son, the couple discovered that the only thing they now had in common was an addiction to alcohol.

The situation reached crisis point when Frank woke up one day and felt that he had had enough. In his view, his mild manner was being mistaken for weakness of character and he decided to cut all ties by removing himself totally from the toxic marital environment. He bundled his belongings into a suitcase, headed for California and started afresh. The abandoned wife would, at some point afterwards, petition for divorce. It was not contested, but Frank sought and was granted access to the couple's son. He maintained his contact entitlement by returning to Chicago at specific arranged times. He would book into a hotel and spend several days with his boy, often taking him to various outdoor activities, including fishing trips.

Meanwhile, secure in his confirmed permanent status in the United States, Frank went on to build a new life as a single, unattached American citizen in the state of California. He found himself a studio apartment and experienced no difficulty in finding employment as a hotel Bellboy. It was the job he knew well and had become accustomed to. Moreover, hotels of the era were at all times in need of Bellboys. But Frank had been considered reliably competent, amiable and well-liked, and as a consequence was given "grand status" by being made Head Bellboy! Even so, Frank, whose dream of becoming a Medical Doctor had been dashed, desired a more worthwhile occupation, and he enrolled on an Engineering Course at a local college. On completion, he applied to fill the advertised vacancy as Head of Occupations at his place of work. His application was successful and he retained the post for many years up to his retirement.

Frank was in a good place. He had adjusted fully into his new life in California, but something was missing. He was divorced from his wife and had been focusing on establishing a career. He now held a satisfying work position and was enjoying the single life and being free to drink and smoke in his apartment to his heart's content. In spite of the positives derived from being unattached, Frank knew that he could not carry on indefinitely with his indulgent life-style and seriously considered finding himself a significant other. Consequently, when he became attracted to a new female employee who carried a pronounced physical disability, Frank decided to follow his instincts. He discovered, in due course, that the person of interest was pleasant and outgoing. She had a beautiful smile and engaged with him in a warm and friendly manner. Before too long, the couple were dating, and Frank was convinced that he had at last met his "soul mate".

Frank went on to tie the knot for a second time. He could not be more contented. He was sure that his decision to remarry had been right, and within two years an infant boy was produced. Despite the happy union, Frank was disheartened that his new wife was being targeted because of the large protruding hump on her back. Nonetheless, the family ignored the taunts and continued with their happy life. All the while, Frank was continuing to have meaningful contact with his first son. The brothers were at some point told of each other's existence, prior to being brought together within a family setting.

Domestic bliss continued for a considerable period before the couple gradually grew apart and the marriage eventually collapsed. Frank very much regretted being separated from his family, but came to the conclusion that, although he liked the idea of marriage, he may not be suited to it. "After all, it was not for everyone." Frank decided against marrying for a third time, but never relinquished his parental responsibilities. He remained a doting father and was alleged to have spoiled both sons "rotten".

Although he stuck to his pledge by never remarrying, Frank would move on to developing a serious long-standing relationship with a charismatic woman who walked with a limp as a result of a "club foot". Eyebrows were again curiously raised. "Why do you always pick women that are either hugely overweight or have some form of disability?" Frank acknowledged that he was indeed drawn to females who were not conventionally attractive, but insisted that not "everything" about them was that way. His reply may have been indicative of a man who looked beyond the physical imperfections and discovered the beauty within.

Although Frank had created a new life in the United States, thoughts of home remained. Even though he was initially the rejected youngest child, his older siblings had in time grown accustomed to his presence and he became a fully accepted member of the closely connected fold. Consequently, Frank had been haunted by the guilt of severing contact with his family and, in a moment of overwhelming nostalgia, impulsively booked a return and reconnected with the folk back home. It was an emotional reunion. The siblings were overjoyed by the surprise appearance of their long-lost brother and their embraces were heart-felt and lingering. There was plenty of "catching up", and Frank was devastated to learn of the sad losses, in particular the demise of their beloved mother, Angie.

Apart from happy times spent with close family members, Frank travelled the length and breadth of the island. He marvelled at the once "taken for granted" glorious landscapes and visited old friends and familiar places. All too soon the time had come to wave goodbye, and Frank flew back to his life in the United States. The siblings he visited would never again set eyes on their errant little brother.

Frank felt somewhat home-sick after returning to his home in California, but some time subsequently, and out-of-the-blue, his sister Eileen, who resided with her family in London, England, appeared on his door-step! Frank was staggered and totally overcome with emotion. The siblings screamed and fell into each other's arms. It had been the first time they had clapped eyes on each other in more than fifty years and they were ecstatic. Nonetheless, it felt to them both that they were, just yesterday, two little kids, playing hide and seek in the bush, climbing trees or fishing in local rivers and streams. How well they remembered those "good old childhood days". Their short period of reconnection had been euphorically memorable.

The re-appearance of Frank had provided closure for the surviving siblings. The "not knowing" in relation to his welfare had been agonising for them all. And Frank found peace of mind after years of self-inflicted torturous separation from his family. They would never again lose contact with each other.

Frank occupied a studio apartment in the house he owned but rented out in separate apartments. He was, as time went on, known to have struck up a relationship with a young lady, alleged to have been mentally impaired. However, his final years were lived as a recluse, "cooped up" in his studio, drinking and smoking to excess.

"In every life a little rain will fall"; but Frank, alias Thomas Radix, did not linger indefinitely on setbacks or disappointments, and always sought an alternative path. And, by so doing, succeeded in achieving the American Dream, albeit in a manner that had not been predicted or even anticipated. Despite being pleasant and quietly spoken, Frank had been, in essence, a man of considerable depth and possessed of an unbreakable spirit.

At the end of his chequered life journey, Frank passed away in hospital from heart failure. He is remembered fondly by surviving family members.

Thomas Radix
1921-1994

A TALE OF TWO SISTERS

Sisters, Rosie and Eileen, who were seven years apart in age, had been the closest of friends, and always supportive of each other. The sisters shared a home in the city of St George whilst pursuing their separate careers. Rosie owned and managed one of the most popular restaurants in the city of the day. Eileen combined her skills as a seamstress with managing a local Pharmacy owned by her brother, Dr Lincoln.

Flashback twenty or more years. Rosie entered into marriage, for better or worse, anticipating a long and happy life with her new husband and their hoped-for offspring, but it was not to be. Rosie gave little explanation in relation to the breakdown of her marriage, but with emphasis on the word "ring" would only say: "The suffe*ring* followed soon after I got the wedding *ring*." Those who had been privy to the intimate details revealed that the groom, who had been frequently absent from the marital home, eventually ran off with the "other woman" within one year of solemnly vowing "Till Death Do Us Part" at their lavish church wedding. But even though Rosie lost her husband, she did not lose her self-esteem. She rose above the heartbreak, shrugged off feelings of bitter disappointment and betrayal and took on a fatalistic stance. "What will be, will be," she sighed, and simply moved on with her life.

Rosie was a popular figure. Individuals who crossed her path were captivated by her engaging conversations, and warm and generous spirit. Surrounded by an aura of fun, Rosie was a "laugh-a-minute" character with a sharp wit, who could, at the "drop of a hat", pluck a hilariously funny joke from nowhere, resulting in everyone present spontaneously falling into uncontrollable laughter.

Growing up had not been easy for Rosie. She was a sickly baby and not expected to survive beyond a few weeks. But William and Angie were unable to accept the doctors' grim prognosis and refused to give up on their precious daughter. The couple employed a nurse to attend to the child's every need and, along with breast milk from her mother, Rosie was fed a recommended multi-vitamin liquid supplement. The first few years were difficult. Despite receiving the best care and attention, Rosie failed to make significant progress, and alarm bells started ringing when, at aged two, she was still unable to talk, walk or even stand unaided. Consequently, the family were simultaneously shocked and relieved when, suddenly and unexpectedly, Rosie got to her feet and, in strong voice, uttered her first words. She was three years old. She would thereafter develop in leaps and bounds into a healthy, well-built and robust little tom-boy who was quick to flex her muscles. Rosie, in later years, admitted, in triumphant tones, to instigating physical "fights" with her peers on a daily basis after school and that she was always "the winner"!

Rosie performed well at school and, aged twelve, her parents, William and Angie, decided to enable her the opportunity of a Secondary education. The couple applied for a place for their daughter at the prestigious fee-paying St Joseph's Convent, located in the city of St George, and they were delighted on receiving notification of her acceptance. Rosie was ecstatic and bubbling with excitement and told everyone that she would be transferring to the Convent at the beginning of the next term. Meanwhile, she was fitted for the required pleated skirts and white shirts and, before too long, the complete uniform, as well as learning materials, were in place and ready for the "big day". Rosie could hardly wait and counted down the days leading up to when she would be setting-off on the journey to her new school in the city, donning her crisp new uniform and feeling proud. The likelihood of an unforeseen event obstructing a highly anticipated educational future would not have even entered the psyche of this particular twelve-year-old child, or indeed her family.

Rosie had been in the grip of euphoria and looking forward to her first day at St Joseph's Convent, when she was, without warning, stunned by a series of life-changing events. William passed suddenly and unexpectedly after a short illness. The devastating loss of the main breadwinner resulted in the proposed fee-paying education being scrapped. And, as paid domestic helpers were no longer affordable, Rosie was not returned to the local school house. She was now needed at home to assist with the various daily chores as the family pulled together during a period of financial crisis. The educational prospects of this bright and enthusiastic young girl were, as a consequence, being severed at the tender age of twelve. Rosie was heartbroken.

Although Rosie understood well the reasons for being withdrawn from school, it had been, nonetheless, a shockingly cruel jolt into adulthood. But her sadness would be internalised as she "stepped up to the plate" and, without complaining, carried on with every task required. It was not until she was in her early twenties that Rosie expressed regret that she had not been able to continue with her education, or even permitted to join the Girl Guides. She had, nonetheless, been compensated by being provided with piano lessons, at a time when the family's circumstances had improved. Despite being denied the longed-for educational opportunities, Rosie derived personal satisfaction and felt privileged to have played a significant role in supporting her family during their time of need.

The saying, "What does not kill you makes you stronger", could have been applied to Rosie, as she emerged as an independent and enterprising woman with a "strong back", determined to avoid ever again being in the service of others. Consequently, she did not seek employment and became successful as a self-employed business woman, not only in the homeland, but also the neighbouring island of Trinidad.

Eileen was the youngest of three sisters and much favoured by her older siblings. Unlike middle sister, Rosie, who presented no challenges to their mother, Eileen always stood her ground and would demand answers if she felt that she was being treated unfairly. She was, indeed, a wilful child, who rebelled against having to attend school every day, and deliberately ignored her mother's "no dancing" rule by breaking into the Charleston at any given opportunity. She also loved dressing up and wearing pretty ribbons in her hair. And, at aged seven, she was already sewing her very own pretty frocks.

Angie was aghast at her youngest daughter's persistent pattern of disobedience. The child just "will not hear," she fumed, and decided to place her in the care of relatives who resided in the city of St George. "Eileen looks like a bright girl," Angie reasoned. "Let's see how she likes living in town." Not surprisingly, the precocious child was delighted to be told that she would be going to stay with a relative and her twenty-something daughter, who lived in the city. The eight-year-old very much admired the fashionable outfits worn by her older cousin, her styled hair and sparkling personality. Furthermore, the bright young thing of the day was a party girl who loved music and dancing and was, ideally, the kind of woman Eileen dreamt of becoming some-day. Consequently, the fact that she would be part of this fanciful world filled with glitter and glamour had been a wonderful prospect for the starry-eyed little girl.

But it was not long into her new life in the city that Eileen discovered that the reality of living with the "alluring" relatives was not as she imagined it would be. She was not being properly cared for. Her clothing was not laundered. She was fed on scraps or nothing at all and was often hungry and thirsty. Eileen recalled venturing into the nearby market and, with parched lips, was staring longingly at a drinks stall when, all of a sudden, she heard a man's voice saying, "Give her a drink! Give her a big drink!", while handing over coins to the vendor. Eileen claimed it to be the most enjoyable beverage she had ever had and could not thank the kindly stranger enough. Meanwhile, neighbours were becoming increasingly concerned by Eileen's dishevelled and pitiful appearance and sent word to Angie that her daughter was being neglected. Angie was immediately alarmed and wasted no time in arranging Eileen's return to the family home in the sleepy village of Vincennes, St David's.

Eileen was relieved to be back with her family. The unhappy experience had been, for Eileen, a stark realisation that even though her mother was a harsh disciplinarian, her children were always kept clean, appropriately dressed, and above all well fed and watered. It had been undoubtedly a lesson in being careful for what you wish for, and Eileen became noticeably less challenging. But her creativity was not overlooked and she was in time enabled to develop her "God given" talents by being provided with professional training in needlework, dressmaking and embroidery.

After leaving school, Eileen went on to become a reputable seamstress with many customers. She was also a fashion-conscious, attractively dressed and admired young woman. During her twenties, Eileen visited various islands within the region and spent a short period in North America. But the beautiful, vivacious and adventurous young woman found difficulty finding love. Like many women, Eileen felt that her life would not be complete without a good man by her side, and she yearned for marriage and children. After a series of failed romances, time was moving fast, she was getting older and Eileen feared being left on the shelf. But it was when she was at her lowest that she was introduced, by a mutual friend, to the individual who was destined to significantly impact her life. At that point, Eileen believed that she had at last found her Mr Right. Although he was fourteen years her senior and may not have been the most handsome of men, what he lacked in looks was compensated by his intelligence, radiant personality and the fact that he held a high employment position. During the course of their relationship, the couple discovered that they shared an appreciation of music. Both were amateur musicians and often accompanied each other on the piano.

Eileen could not be happier. There was not a doubt in her mind that good things do indeed come to those who wait. She reflected on having kissed plenty of "frogs" on the journey that led to finding her prince, but it had all been "worth it". When, out of the blue, Eileen received a proposal of marriage from the love of her life, she could have exploded with joy and her happiness was shared by family and friends. Life could not be better and she was soon planning the grand wedding she had dreamed of since she was a little girl.

The engagement was followed by many nights' ecstasy and abandoned passions. Consequently, Eileen was not surprised on discovering that she was carrying her fiancé's baby within weeks of their engagement and could hardly wait to share with him the happy coming. But Eileen was unprepared for his response to what she believed would be welcomed news. "Was he just having an off day?" she wondered. "Maybe he needs a day or two to get used to the fact that they would be starting a family sooner than anticipated." However, Eileen became more and more worried and anxious as days and weeks went by without seeing or hearing from the significant other. And her world came crashing down when it came to light that her "dream man", who lived on the other side of the island, was already married with a family! Furthermore, Eileen discovered that he was, in his community, a well-known serial womaniser and that he had fathered children with various women across the land. Shock! Horror! Crushed under the debris of her smashed world, Eileen was rescued by her supportive brothers, and, moreover, her older sister, who dashed to her side and remained there during the most testing period. Eileen, in due course, gave birth to an infant daughter and Rosie, who had no children of her own, would forever play a significant role in caring for the adored child.

Life continued with the sisters and Eileen's daughter residing together under one roof, while jointly participating in the shared care arrangements that had been put into place. It had been a contented period for Rosie. Not only did she cherish the presence of her little niece, but she ran a flourishing business, was in a happy long-term personal relationship, and maintained regular contact with her brothers. O'Hanley and Tox had returned home after a period of living and working abroad, and, apart from Thomas, whose whereabouts were unknown, the family resided in the homeland and the sibling bond remained intact. They were also patriotic sons and daughters of the island of their birth and, despite travelling to foreign countries, never considered living permanently elsewhere.

Fully recovered from the bereavement of being dumped by the man she loved and thinking that she had had a "lucky escape", Eileen focused on her career, and cherished her relationships with close family members and friends. However, there was an underlying restlessness associated with a nagging inner voice that suggested a fate awaited her across the sea. Consequently, when news broke that Britain had opened her doors to English-speaking British West Indians, it had been for Eileen a signal that it was an opportunity not to be missed. It was also rumoured that England was a land of milk and honey. The streets were paved with gold and there were large fortunes to be made.

In reality, Britain had been advertising for workers to fill the large number of vacancies that remained unfilled, particularly within the Transport System and also the National Health. The response was relatively huge, with many embracing the chance of a better life. They included women eager to escape oppressive marriages, unsupported single mothers and large numbers of skilled and unskilled men and women seeking employment. Those with insufficient funds for purchasing a one-way ticket to the "promise land" borrowed from relatives or friends, sold their possessions or scrimped and saved. The majority had no intention of residing permanently in Great Britain and anticipated returning "home" after accumulating enough money to build a "big house". But many children would be left in the care of others as the optimistic seekers of wealth embarked on their once-in-a-life-time journey.

Eileen had been keen to join with other enthusiasts and try her luck by uprooting and starting a new life in the land of plenty. She was, however, determined that she would not be travelling without sister Rosie by her side. Rosie was hesitant about giving up her happy and relatively successful life for the unknown. She was, after all, in her middle years and was strongly of the opinion that this opening into a new and better life would be more appropriate for younger people or skilled or unskilled individuals seeking greater opportunities. Moreover, Rosie's boyfriend, a well-known market vendor, had been totally against the idea. Like Rosie, he did not believe it was for them, and the couple refused to be swayed by the general hype. It all seemed too good to be true. But Eileen remained persistent, and eventually, with heavy heart and still not convinced, Rosie agreed, reluctantly, to sell up the business, put her relationship on hold, and support her sister by accompanying her into the unknown. There was, nonetheless, one proviso: "If it doesn't work for me, I'm coming straight back!" Rosie asserted firmly.

The day finally arrived when the sisters, with their little girl in tow, joined hundreds of other hopefuls and boarded an Italian schooner headed for a far-away land that lay beyond the Atlantic Ocean. But while everyone chatted noisily and excitedly about the highly anticipated opportunities, Rosie remained quietly pessimistic.

Following a journey of several weeks and stop-offs in Spain and Italy, the schooner docked at Dover, England, and the passengers were transferred onto a train and taken to Victoria Station, London. There to meet the family was a relative and her husband. The couple were early post-war immigrants and had been residing in West London for a number of years. The sisters seized the opportunity of taking in some of the sights of London as they were being transported by taxi to the relatives' apartment. They were impressed by pairs of young policemen, smartly dressed in uniform and caps, strolling on pavements. They admired with interest historic grey buildings and glimpsed at ancient churches, and at least one majestic-looking cathedral, as the taxi drove through main roads that were congested with motor vehicles, or side roads that contained riders on bicycles or motorcycles. One of the main attractions was the red Route-master buses, but while Eileen imagined sitting on the top deck of a bus for a better view ahead, Rosie had been quick to observe litter being swept away by the city's road sweepers. Even though she knew well that the rumour, the streets of London were "paved with gold", had been an analogy in relation to overall prosperity, she was unable to resist quipping in sarcastic tones, "They must have collected up all the gold before we arrived!"

After being provided with a meal at the relatives' apartment, the sisters were taken to a tenement house on a tree-lined street, on which children played noisily and happily. They were informed that it was where "a room" had been secured by a paid deposit, pending their arrival. The newcomers were initially struck by the fact that the building was at least five stories high but hoped that they would not be placed at the very top. However, after a laboured climb up a "never-ending" stairwell, the sisters were shocked to discover that their room was actually the attic! But there was more to come. They were informed that the house did not have a bathroom, and the one and only toilet, shared by the various rooming tenants, was located on the middle floor. They were, however, reassured that bathing and laundry facilities were available at a fee within the locality.

Rosie and Eileen were dissatisfied with the limited basic resources and decided to seek alternative accommodation. They would, however, discover, after a string of house moves, that affordable rental accommodation within the North Kensington area of London of the period had been much of a muchness. It was essentially a poor area and many people lived in privately rented sub-standard accommodation with shared facilities or outdoor toilets, and that public baths had been the accepted norm. It was not unusual to find that some "Rooms to Let" notices specified No Blacks. No Irish. No Dogs. "At least we know we're not wanted here. Saves a lot of embarrassment," was Rosie's usually matter-of-fact response. Rented rooms did not come with heating and, dressed in extra layers, everyone hovered around a paraffin heater placed at the centre of the room and shivered during cold winter months. And, due to the limited facilities, buckets with lids were purchased for storing water, basins were used for washing and the mandatory "potty" was at all times concealed beneath the bed.

It was an era when the majority food-shopped on a daily basis at corner shops or greengrocers. These outlets operated from Monday to Saturday, on a tight 9am to 5.30pm schedule, and Caribbean varieties such as sweet potatoes, yams, plantain and avocado were not stocked. However, at a time when kitchens were shared with other renters, the preparation of large meals was not considered a viable option. And, subsequent to slotting a "one-shilling" coin into the gas meter, necessary for obtaining their quota of gas, the women would quickly rustle-up a meal consisting of rice and beans, or rice and some form of canned fish. Fish and chips, purchased from the local fish and chip shop, and wrapped in discarded newspapers, had been the regular Friday-night treat. Meals were often washed down with tea brewed in a tea-pot and poured into the cup through a strainer. Adopted from the host nation, the sisters enjoyed the warming, comforting and reviving benefits of the nation's favourite beverage. "Nothing better than a nice cup of tea," Rosie often remarked, while supping her favourite brew.

In an age when "Best Before", "Sell By" or "Use By" did not appear on packaged foods or bottled drinks, and in the absence of a refrigerator, draughty window-sills had been, for the sisters, the ideal place for preserving the freshness of milk and other perishables.

There was an overall resentment of Caribbean people, particularly by those among the struggling working classes who may have lived next door to the unwelcome immigrants. Many West Indians alleged being verbally abused or even spat upon. And it was not uncommon to hear of individual black men being physically attacked at night time. Significant numbers within the indigenous population felt that West Indians had come to take their jobs or wanted to cash in on State Benefits. And negative comments relating to the arrival of immigrant British West Indians to the United Kingdom were expressed by named Members of Parliament. The fact that these people had been invited into the country to fill the employment gap may have been overlooked, but new arrivals from the Caribbean were made to feel unwelcomed and may even have been viewed as being the new under-class.

In spite of the projected hostility, there could be no denying that the country needed economic migrants. It was a time when application forms were not generally required and vacancies were often filled via word of mouth or displayed notices. There were those who joined work-forces that were required to clock in and clock out, at the beginning and end of the working day, and alterations to wages earned were made accordingly. Information in relation to income, hours worked and deductions would be documented at the front of the weekly pay packet. But migrants were taken on as workers in motoring plants, as bus conductors, guards on the underground and railway, kitchen assistants in hotels and restaurants, and various lowly paid jobs that no-one else wanted to do. At the other end of the scale, many aspiring young Caribbean women of the day found employment as State-Enrolled Nurses in National Health hospitals, with the more ambitious progressing to becoming State-Registered Nurses.

Eileen and Rosie had been among the pioneer generation who arrived in Britain during the post-war era up to the 1970s. It had been the first time that people from different islands in the Caribbean found themselves living side by side in Britain. They were intrigued by each other's separate sub-cultures and unique accents and dialects of English and French Patios, which were not always mutually understood. There was also an imposed hierarchy. The Jamaicans were confident and could be fearlessly challenging in their interactions. They considered themselves superior and more enlightened than those from the smaller islands, known as "smallies". The Trinidadians boasted that they were the "tops" because of their carnival tradition; and, of course, the island produced oil. The "Bajans" felt that they were better educated. Furthermore, they were proud that Barbados was known as "Little England", due to the large number of English visitors to the island. In spite of the banter and jostle for status, West Indians had been well aware that they were immigrants from the same part of the world and should therefore stick together and may even have been strengthened and buoyed by their shared sense of comradeship. In reality, they were essentially all on the same level.

Having an open and welcoming home had been a way of life carried over from the Caribbean. The immigrant community felt free to visit each other whenever they wished and, despite the surrounding hostility, were happy within their bubble. There were plenty of house parties and "blues dances", where everyone was welcome, and if revellers were not boogying-on-down in time with the beat, held tightly to a chosen partner and swooned dreamily to soulful rhythms. At the end of an exhilarating night of partying, the majority would hurry home for a few hours of restful sleep, before waking for church on Sunday morning.

Rosie and Eileen were not members of the social scene. But while Eileen enjoyed the music of the day, as far as Rosie was concerned, there was no better sound than the melodic rhythms of American Country. And she was often heard, in high-pitched tones, belting out her favourite country songs while they were being played on the radio.

Eileen had been one of thousands of immigrants from the Caribbean who, instead of looking back with regret, decided to grab the nettle and forge ahead. She remained optimistic and never lost the feeling that all would be well in the end. She looked forward to visiting places of interest, such as Buckingham Place, the British Museum and Madame Tussauds. Enamoured by Royalty, and the Queen in particular, Eileen was thrilled to see Buckingham Palace for the first time. She enjoyed attending Fun Fairs. The Roller-Coaster had been her favourite ride and she would hold her head back and scream loudly all through the pleasurable but scary stomach-churning, sharply-taken twists, turns and dips. But, hopping onto and sitting on the upper-deck of a red Routemaster and being able to enjoy a scenic ride was not as Eileen anticipated it would be. She discovered that the upper deck was a smoke-filled environment, with plenty of coughing. But she was, nonetheless, fascinated by the bus conductor, with his little ticket machine strapped to his chest, calling out, "Fares, please. Fares, please." Eileen alleged that, due to the "fog", she did not see him coming until he was "right above" her. It was, however, a period when smoking was "cool" and the public were largely unaware of the dangers in relation to smoking and smoke inhalation.

Many people who had arrived from the Caribbean with established careers found that it was almost impossible to find employment in their chosen field. Eileen, however, could not have been happier when she was eventually successful in obtaining a reasonably paid job as a seamstress, an occupation in which she was already skilled. Moreover, she was placed in a team that included several other Caribbean women and led to the development of long-lasting meaningful friendships.

Eileen also formed new friendships with other newcomers in the neighbourhood in which she lived, one of whom happened to be a handsome, well-presented young man with a quiet demeanour. As their friendship grew, the couple discovered that they had feelings for each other. They began spending more and more time together, and Eileen found herself falling in love. Although it was an emotion over which she had no control, Eileen was both cautious and fearful. She recalled her previous experience of being in a serious relationship which ended so disastrously. Could she trust this person? The thought of her heart being shattered for a second time was unbearable. But Eileen chose to continue with the relationship and hoped for the very best outcome. She would not be disappointed. Eileen had been assured that she had at last found her prince on the day her suitor proposed marriage. She was elated. Life could not have been better.

And so it was, within two years of taking a chance on a new life in the mother country, Eileen was married to the love of her life, had a perfect job and was soon expecting a baby. Three children in total would be produced from the marriage. In spite of the daily routines of work, combined with the responsibilities of raising a family and the ups and downs of the marital relationship, Eileen knew that she had found herself a good husband. He was, throughout the marriage, responsible, loyal and dependable, and their offspring were raised in a stable and secure environment.

While Eileen's high anticipation of a better life in the United Kingdom had been unfolding as expected, at the other end of the spectrum, Rosie's pessimism regarding the promised good life in London had, for her, been rightly predicted. Unlike Eileen, she did not slot easily into employment. She had been at all times self-employed and, without a specific skill, could do nothing but accept lowly paid menial jobs such as washing-up dishes and cleaning kitchens in eating houses, which were tasks undertaken by employees at the restaurant she owned and managed in the homeland. Once a big fish in a small pool, Rosie now found that she was a very small and insignificant fish in a large pool.

Things were not going well for Rosie. She was depressed and downhearted and sought solace from cigarettes. But it was while she was at her lowest ebb that Rosie's life began an upward turn. She was offered a position as head of the laundry room at a well-known hotel in Park Lane. She was effective in the role and became a trusted and popular member of staff. Meanwhile, Rosie had been making links with individuals within her local community and was a respected member of the supportive network of friends. But even though she had in various ways adjusted to her new life, happy memories of "home" lingered. In particular, Rosie missed the good man she had left behind. Would she find a replacement? That was debateable. But a second marriage was, for certain, out of the question. Rosie did not waver in her "never again" and "once bitten, twice shy" mind-set. Nonetheless, there were no shortage of admirers, and she may have eventually moved on, romantically, with the resolve that, if you can't be with the one you love, you might as well love the one you are with.

Many West Indians of the period would support each other by pooling their money within a disciplined system called "Partner" by some and "Sui Sui" by others. It required a group of six or more individuals paying-in a collectively agreed amount of money each week to the Co-ordinator, and the total sum collected would be paid out, in turn, to each member of the group. Members often used "Partner" savings for specific purposes, such as payment on a deposit for purchasing a house, or an airline ticket that would enable a close family member or love interest to join them in the United Kingdom. The initial intention of returning "home" after quickly accumulating "big money" had become a far-off goal, having been faced with the reality of the economic up-hill climb.

Subsequent to taking the decision to put into place her very own savings system, Rosie enlisted ten participants, including herself. It was all going to plan and running smoothly, but somewhere down the line the group was scammed by a rogue member and, in her role as Co-ordinator, Rosie held responsibility for settling the outstanding debt. The unfortunate episode would signal the end of her involvement in further similar schemes.

The "Partner" method of saving, nonetheless, remained popular among pioneer West Indians, and many were enabled to purchases houses. In those days, a large radiogram had been the prize possession and considered rightfully deserving of its prominent position in the cramped little sitting room. These lounges had been, in the main, no-go areas, designed to be admired by visitors but entered only on special occasions. They were often decorated with brightly coloured and flowery wallpaper, matching curtains and bold-patterned carpets. The furniture consisted of two-seater-cushioned settees adorned with crochet backrests and coffee tables with centred crochet doilies. See-through cabinets were filled with assortments of pretty dining sets, tea-cups and saucers and drinking glasses. Numerous little ornaments were placed at various places, and framed family photographs hung from the walls.

Prior to immigrating, Rosie and Eileen shared a house together and were supportive of each other, but Rosie had been the main carer of her niece. The joint living arrangements were maintained after the sisters' arrival in London and continued, albeit with appropriate modification, after Eileen had married and started a new family. Furthermore, Rosie had no intention of relinquishing her shared parenting role in relation to the niece that came to represent the child she never had.

The years evolved and the sisters settled into their separate daily routines, which involved supporting each other with work and family commitments. However, they continued to write and receive letters from the family back home and were visited for weeks at a time by various members of the sibling group.

Even though Rosie and Eileen resided with their family in the area that was central to the fledgling Notting Hill Carnival, they were not involved in the festivities attended mainly by the minority West Indian population that lived around London. It had been, no less, two days of the year when they felt enabled to embrace their music culture. And, alongside costumed bands, revellers would let themselves go and in abandoned fashion gyrate to the pulsating and intoxicating beat of steel drums as they progressed through narrow streets within the area.

Although the transformation into a situation of having to start her life all over again had been difficult, Rosie had arrived at a place of acceptance. She had sacrificed a good life for the sake of her sister, but she no longer ached over what she had left behind. "Such is life," she told herself, with a sigh of resignation. "Just have to make the best of what you have." But it would be without warning that Rosie was delivered the shock that would result in a single-minded reassessment of her life.

Apart from being a life-long sufferer of migraine, Rosie always believed that her basic health was good. She was completely unaware the "silent killer" Hypertension had been tightening its grip, until, after returning home from work one evening, Rosie was standing in the kitchen preparing a meal when she was suddenly and unexpectedly struck down by a stroke. An ambulance was called and she was transported to hospital, where she remained for several weeks. The illness had been, for Rosie, a wake-up call. While lying in her hospital bed, she decided that the time had come to put her own needs before those of others. And if it was God's Will that she survived, she would, without delay, return home for good. Rosie's prayers were answered. She made a full recovery, was discharged from hospital and, within a short period of time and in spite of being urged by her sister to reconsider her decision, Rosie stuck to her guns and booked a one-way flight to the Caribbean. While acknowledging that England had been beneficial to the majority of immigrants, Rosie felt convinced that her initial hunch that it was not the place for her had been right and wished she had listened to her gut.

Rosie would experience no regrets returning home. Indeed, she found a sense of peace and contentment that had been absent throughout the period spent in the United Kingdom. She refused to lament on what could have been if she had not taken the life-changing decision to accompany her sister on the quest to a better life. Instead, she would hit the ground running and with optimism. Rosie's siblings who lived on the island had been over-the-moon to have her back, and she was welcomed into the home of her elder sister, Clarice, who had by then re-established herself after returning from the United States and had opened up a retail outlet in the city of St George. Rosie joined in the business following her arrival and managed day-to-day operations. Clarice, meanwhile, stayed at home and focused her energies on caring for Aunt Evie.

On days that she was not working, Rosie would spend much of her time reconnecting with old friends. However, a meeting with the boyfriend who was left behind had been her priority. After making contact, the couple arranged to see each other at what used to be their favourite venue. It was a heartfelt reunion and the evening was spent reminiscing on past times; but, as their conversation progressed into the current, Rosie discovered that her "one-time" partner had moved on with someone else. Despite being momentarily disappointed, the information was not unexpected, and, with an expression of resignation, she responded with the words, "Such is life." But she wished him well and the pair remained life-long friends. Rosie was not known to have had a subsequent serious relationship.

Time marched on, and Rosie and Clarice arrived at a stage when they both agreed that they should give up the relatively hectic life of the city and re-locate to the serenity of the countryside. The sisters moved into a property owned by Clarice in the parish of St David's, where they had been born and raised, and very soon opened up a Convenience Store within their small community. During the ensuing period, Rosie and Clarice received visits from family members who resided in England and also America. Rosie would visit London once, for a few short weeks, following her decision to return to her old life in the homeland.

Rosie became integral to the slow-moving country community in which she lived. Her customers were served with a smiling face, and at a no-hurry, no-worry pace, while she puffed intermittently on the cigarette that seemed to be forever clutched between her fingers. She readily engaged in conversation and often responded with humour to the juicy gossip of the day. While Rosie was leisurely serving and happily interacting with customers, Clarice was busily looking after the house, garden and animals, but operated a schedule that ensured meals being cooked and ready to be eaten at regular times each day. Shop was shut on Sunday and the sisters, dressed in elegant outfits, would accompany each other to the morning Mass being held at a nearby church. Afternoons may be spent entertaining guests or engaging in separate social activities. Rosie had been of calm character and was rarely ruffled, and she chose to ignore the short but heated outbursts of her volatile sister. Essentially, however, the women related well with each other, and enjoyed each other's company.

The sisters lived in a community where incidents of crime had been either very low or non-existent. But even though their brothers maintained regular contact with them and were vigilant, the women, who were growing older, decided to take additional precautionary measures for protecting their safety. In so doing, they employed a seemingly fearless, well-built young man for providing overnight security.

Feeling safe and secure in the knowledge that their protector occupied a bedroom in the house, the sisters drifted into slumber one night, but were abruptly awoken in the early hours of the following morning by a burglar. Rosie and Clarice screamed for help as they were being beaten around the head, but the security that had been put into place failed to act in their defence. In fact, he was nowhere to be seen and could not be heard. The intruder eventually escaped, having stolen all the money he was able to lay his hands on and various pieces of jewellery. The sisters were shocked and bruised and pondering the whereabouts of the young man who had been paid to protect them, when he was spotted emerging precariously from beneath the bed as they entered his room. The women were stunned. The "beefy" protector had been in reality a coward, concerned only with saving himself! Rosie was quietly dumbfounded, but Clarice was furious. She erupted into a tirade of angry words which culminated in the "shame-faced" deceptive individual being given his marching orders.

The incident was reported to the police, but the matter was dropped following a futile investigation. Essentially, the women were unable to identify their attacker, but it was generally assumed that he was from a far-away parish. However, the robbery had been fossil fuel for sensationalised hot gossip that excited the lives of those who resided in the normally dull and uneventful community.

Although somewhat shaken, the women had in time picked up the pieces and continued their daily routines. But they were reassured that their brothers' vigilance had been stepped up and a watchful eye was being pledged by various individuals who lived locally. Even though Rosie recovered fully from her sustained physical injuries, there can be no doubting that the mental scars remained. Nonetheless, she appeared to have been moving on contentedly when, without warning, she suffered a second stroke and fell into unconsciousness shortly after getting out of bed one morning. She was immediately rushed to hospital, but efforts at resuscitation failed. It had been seventeen years since suffering her first stroke.

Family and friends were devastated by the loss of this much-loved mother-figure, sister, aunt, cousin and friend, who never hesitated in putting the needs of others before those of her own, and willingly went that extra mile, although some may say that the inability to say "no" had been the problem she carried and was never relieved from. Despite the related lack of assertiveness, Rosie had nonetheless been a strong and independent woman, who overcame life's challenges and boldly achieved her goals.

Rosie's light was extinguished instantaneously and peacefully during a relaxed and tranquil period in her life. She would have had no regrets. She is remembered with affection for her sharp wit, warm heart, generous spirit, and considerable fortitude.

Following Rosie's departure, Eileen carried on with her life in London. Indeed, the decision to begin a new chapter in the United Kingdom had been right for her. She found happiness in her marriage and raised her family within a stable and secure home. She was a loving and devoted mother who gave up her job as a seamstress and obtained employment as a Home Carer. This enabled the flexibility to combine work with family commitments. Despite receiving a weekly housekeeping allowance from her husband, Eileen was a thrifty and independent woman who was determined to earn her own money. But, unbeknown to her spouse, of every pound earned, 50% of the housekeeping was saved into her secret personal bank account. She used her excellent budgeting techniques and sewing skills to ensure that the siblings were appropriately clothed, the cupboards were at all times filled with food and snacks, and hot, nourishing meals were being provided on a daily basis.

Eileen was a jolly and sociable individual, with a ready smile, and who would collapse with hysterical laughter when relating humorous stories. She was always practically helpful to others, loved entertaining visitors and welcomed staying visits from overseas relatives. In particular, "Aunt Eileen" was, on a regular basis, visited by the various young nieces and nephews who studied at universities in Ireland and England. Among them was Kenrick Radix and his close friend Maurice Bishop, who were at the time both studying Law. Eileen was deeply interested in "back-home" politics and often engaged with them in heated discussions and debates on various related issues. She would have had no idea that seeds were being sewn for what would result in historical political interventions and end in national tragedy.

Eileen was widowed after 40 years of marriage but remained physically active and carried on working well beyond retirement. She was, throughout her life, a strong, determined and independently minded woman who continued to be self-caring during her later years. She disliked using washing machines because, in her opinion, they did not wash clothing and bedding "clean enough". Consequently, laundry would always be undertaken by hand, even at an advanced age, and she insisted on setting and achieving small goals on a daily basis. Always a religious woman, Eileen attended her local church on a regular basis and was well known and respected within the religious community. She was also well read, maintained a keen interest in current affairs and was always up for an argument. She never held back in strongly expressing steadfast opinions, which often resulted in the other side "throwing in the towel" in exasperation, having not been allowed "a word in"! Eileen's offspring had been mindful and respectful of her independent spirit and would never even consider challenging their mother; which, they knew, would result in an outraged and stern response. There are those who might say that Eileen's children were afraid of her. However, the siblings had been secure in the knowledge that, despite commanding respect, their best interests had been, unwaveringly, their mother's top priority.

In spite of her advancing years, Eileen's zest for living was never diminished. She held on tightly and made the best of each day by maintaining a set routine, which included some form of activity like dress-making or taking long walks. She also enjoyed reflecting on the past and often spoke with pride, affection and humour regarding her origins and childhood experiences. Eileen remained in an upbeat frame of mind and very much hoped to recover fully from a stomach complaint, but it was not to be. She passed peacefully in her sleep while being treated in hospital.

Eileen had been a focused and hard-working woman with an adventurous spirit. She found happiness in family life, but always reached out to others. She is remembered fondly for her supportive nature, jolly demeanour and prudence. Eileen had been steadfastly loyal and overwhelmingly proud of her heritage. This strong sense of roots and worth was passed on to her offspring and is being carried forward.

BELIEVE AND ACHIEVE

Alban believed that he was special from childhood. He had been, for a time, the last of eight surviving sons, and he may have been convinced that it was by divine decree that he had been born into what he considered a privileged position among the siblings and revelled in being spoilt by everyone within the household. Consequently, Alban was sorely disappointed and angry when, after four years, his position was lost to the baby brother that had not been anticipated. Alban resented little Thomas for abruptly and unceremoniously stealing his "crown", and would take revenge by pinching, kicking or punching him at any given opportunity for several years subsequent to his birth. Alban would, however, eventually come to terms with having a younger brother and even though he had been "dethroned", Alban's inherent sense of superiority was never lost, and he would, without doubt, have recognised the advantages in relation to being the senior sibling.

On limited occasions when the siblings were allowed to venture out of doors, Alban engaged enthusiastically with neighbourhood boys in activities such as hiking, swimming and cricket. But it had been on their mother's insistence that, when the children were not attending school, church or a specific organised activity, they should be at home. Consequently, Alban found plenty of time to indulge his hobby of reading and, in particular, broadening his knowledge of British Law, which had become his focus of interest. He was fascinated with the subject and as he grew older never missed an opportunity to "bend the ears" of others with his impromptu outpourings on British Legislation, delivered with an air of importance and in a peculiar "put-on", upper-crust English accent. His audience was often amused by the theatre of his highly held head that swung from side to side during passionately delivered speeches. But they were also baffled by his choice of "big words" and amazed that this young lad, from a rural community, who had never even set foot in the United Kingdom, could speak with such precision and conviction. Very few people had been aware that Alban's information had been obtained from various magazines, books, encyclopaedias and the stationery dictionary, all supplied by his father, William and was, in general, considered a pretentious young man and dismissed as being an egotistical dreamer.

Alban was not "put off" by what others thought about him, and his self-esteem was never diminished. As he grew older, he became fastidious about his appearance and demanded that his clothing was impeccably laundered. He was at all times smartly dressed in crisp white shirts, sharply creased trousers and polished shoes, and carried himself well. If he was ever absent from home at meal times, he expected that his share of food would be dished out without spillage on a large plate, covered and placed on a tray, pending his arrival. Alban's unwavering projections of self-belief, captivating charisma and being good at everything had been compelling qualities. And he was, as a consequence, selected to lead every group or organisation he joined up to, including being appointed Head Scout and being voted in as Head Boy at the school he attended. When it was suggested to William and Angie that Alban should achieve highly in his adult life, the couple remained doubtful. Persuaded by Alban's deep Religious Faith, dedication in his role as Altar Boy and his linguistic attributes, both parents were of the opinion that their son would be the first in the family to become a Roman Catholic priest. Moreover, they had been fully aware that beneath the grandiose persona lay a compassionate soul who loved his family and his community and was at heart caring, considerate and at all times willing to offer a helping hand to others.

At the end of a successful school career, Alban went on to become a highly respected teacher at the local school. In spite of the warm climate, he felt the need to reflect his status by never failing to turn up for work smartly dressed in jacket and tie. He was judged to be an effective communicator and conscientious in his desire to promote the importance of education within the local community.

Although Alban derived considerable work satisfaction from teaching and mentoring his young students, he did not feel that he was being fully stretched. Consequent to his abiding interest in British Law, Alban decided that he may be better suited to a career in Law. Although Angie and her late husband had assumed that Alban would have joined the priesthood, she was nonetheless supportive of her son's expressed career choice. The siblings were also delighted and, reassured by the positive responses, Alban successfully gained access to a Law School in the United States of America. No-one doubted that their studious and focused brother and son would in due course realise his ultimate aspiration.

During the period that he studied abroad, Alban maintained regular contact, in the form of letter-writing, with the family at home and received financial support from his better-off older brothers. His sister Clarice, who was at the time working in New York, also played her part by contributing to Alban's training expenses.

The family's combined efforts of support had been rewarded on the day that Alban returned as a fully qualified Lawyer. They were all so proud. Angie was particularly grateful that her son had arrived "in one piece" and fell on her knees in a prayer of thanksgiving. Alban's success was marked with a party attended by relatives and invited guests. It was a joyous occasion, with plenty of food and drinks, punctuated by unexpected hefty but congratulatory thumps on his increasingly bruised back. But, despite the discomfort, the spirit of the occasion was not lost, and a jolly time was being had by everyone present. Prior to the end of the celebration, someone asked for silence and Alban stepped forward and delivered a "thank you" speech. It was received with bemusement and raised eyebrows as guests were increasingly aware that Alban had ditched his one-time "put on" British accent and was now speaking with an acquired jazzy American "twang"!

Alongside the showy and pompous persona, Alban was smartly attired, with an up-right stance and a gait that were reflective of a self-assured man. His cup overflowed with a high sense of hard-earned accomplishment and would burst into exhilaration with the words, "Never felt better in my life!" In spite of the self-obsessed demeanour, underneath was a deeply conscientious heart that was concerned about the welfare of others. Alban wanted to make a difference and in so doing dabbled in politics, while at the same time making his very own personal contributions. Alban provided advice or legal representation to those from poor communities for a minimum fee or, in particular cases, no fee.

Despite being dedicated to his work, Alban pursued various interests and hobbies. He was involved in the local Scout movement, was a keen amateur photographer and an avid reader. Alban was also a strong swimmer, who began each day by completing an energising and refreshing few lengths in cool open waters. Alban maintained close links with his siblings and was fond of his nieces and nephews. Several nephews had been taken under his wing, and apart from engaging them in his various activities, Alban would enquire into their progress at school and provide advice or assistance where appropriate. The youngsters were also welcomed at his offices and he would willingly and enthusiastically reply to all questions relating to the practice.

Alban loved family life. He had been brought up within a large and stable family environment and was genuinely fond of children. But even though he doted on his nieces and nephews, Alban hoped that he would one day marry and raise a family of his own. However, in spite of being introduced to a variety of young women, and had gone on to develop several relationships, he was yet to find that "special someone". But life was good, and even though he applied plenty of effort in everything he did, Alban was mindful of counting his blessings. Meanwhile, he was becoming well known in the region for his expertise as a practising Lawyer, and that may have been the reason he was called upon to act for the Prosecution on a particular case on the neighbouring island of St Vincent. Although he responded positively to the request, it was Alban's intention to return to his practice in the homeland. But the future is unknown, and Alban was oblivious to the fact that fate had intervened and he was being steered onto a new and unanticipated life path.

Alban was no stranger to St Vincent. It had been among the islands he visited with his Scout group as a young boy, and was one of his favourite places. Consequently, he very much looked forward to once again stepping onto St Vincent's lush shores. Subsequent to arrival, and taking up his temporary legal position, Alban quickly adjusted to his new surroundings and was heartened by the warm welcome. He was, nevertheless, focused on the challenge that was placed before him and determined to prove his effectiveness and professionalism.

Having spectacularly won his case, Alban quickly gained recognition and was being bombarded with requests for his services. He was at the same time receiving invites to various social events and gatherings, and it appeared that Alban's contemporaries had been won over, not only by his expertise, but also his attractive personal qualities. It had been an irresistibly seductive environment. Alban abandoned himself to the flow and postponed the return date to his practice back home. There was, however, a life-changing twist, when he was introduced to an attractive young lady with whom he was instantly smitten. The saying, "it never rains unless it pours", may have been applicable, but shortly after meeting what Alban considered the woman of his dreams, he found that he was being drawn to another equally beautiful woman! Following a considerable period of drought, his love-life was all of a sudden flourishing, and Alban gave into temptation by exploiting the situation. He did not initially register a preference but pursued both objects of affection with urgency and vigour. It seemed, at the time, a tonic to his ego that the women were equally responsive to his attentions, and he may have thought of himself as somewhat of a catch; confirmed, no doubt, by the good-looking and well-groomed reflection that was so admired in the mirror.

Although, for a while, Alban had been involved in separate relationships with two beautiful ladies, he eventually came to a decision with regard to a life-partner. But he was unexpectedly knocked back by the stunning revelation that the girl he intended leaving behind had fallen pregnant with his child. Alban was thrown into emotional turmoil and struggled with his conscience. He wanted to do right by his unborn child but was torn between two women. Alban would in time decide to follow his heart, and while pledging support and assistance to the mother-to-be, he would marry the woman of his choosing.

Alban's new wife, who was called Eileen, had been accepting of the circumstances in relation to the child that was yet to be born, and pledged her support. In due course, Alban became the proud father of an infant daughter. A son was produced from the marriage just twelve months subsequently. And so, it was, within a short period of time, Alban's life had been transformed from being single with no dependants to being married and a father of two. He had arrived at a significant turning point, and the initial plan of returning home became a distant memory as Alban embarked on a new life as a family man on the island of St Vincent. He was being led, by the hand of fate, on what would be an impactful and historical journey.

Despite the change of location, there was no change in Alban's magnanimous approach to life. After a relatively short period of taking up permanent residence in St Vincent, he organised the closure of his offices in Grenada and opened up a brand-new practice within his new locality. Alban would in time gain the reputation of being a highly successful lawyer and, as a consequence, was called upon to represent clients in Court Rooms throughout his adopted land. He was, at the same time, widely commended for his altruism. As was the case in Grenada, Alban endeavoured to be of help to those who struggled, and willingly represented the less fortunate in society in return for very little payment. Individuals who existed on the poverty line received his assistance, free of cost. There was nevertheless no discrepancy in his application of diligence and commitment, and he became known as the "poor people's lawyer".

Alban's interests in raising standards within disadvantaged communities was also carried over into his new life. He became a part-time Scout Master and used his status as a vehicle for mentoring young boys. Essentially, Alban was tireless in his efforts to make lives better for the disadvantaged. Indeed, various young individuals within the local community and beyond expressed gratitude to Alban for his guidance, educational assistance, getting a foot on the ladder and generally opening doors into career opportunities. Despite being continually altruistic, Alban remained an impeccably dressed, flamboyant character with an exaggerated positive sense of self, and exuded an aura of confidence. He spoke with perfect diction, albeit with a "showy" American accent, but his warm and caring side shone through and he was fully embraced by the host nation.

Alban maintained a happy family life with his wife, their son and his daughter, who enjoyed periods of staying in contact at the family home. But the nurturing of the sibling relationship had been a priority for the couple and a close bond was developed between them. Due to his concern for disadvantaged families who lived within the locality, Alban and his wife adopted three children and fostered three more, resulting in a total of eight little ones in the often noisy and chaotic, but at all times happy, household. But even though the siblings had been aware that Alban was without doubt their father, he was nonetheless called "Uncle" by them all. As a parent, Alban was described as being loving but strict. The children's education had been a priority for him and he dedicated particular periods for providing assistance with their school-work. They were expected to achieve well and if end-of-term reports did not indicate hard work and progress, particular individuals would be suitably punished.

Despite having a friendly and sociable persona and being actively involved in various outdoor activities, there were occasions when Alban needed to be alone. As a means of ensuring private space, he allocated himself a separate room in the house where he was known to retire, accompanied only by a bottle of his favourite tipple. The consumption of alcohol may have been quenching to a deep-seated personal need, but Alban would become increasingly dependent on the intoxicating beverage. There was always a flask tucked discreetly into his back pocket, from which he sipped during the course of his working day. However, his drinking habit did not appear to have affected his mental capacities, and he remained professionally competent.

An early-morning swim had been a long-standing daily ritual. Alban, who had been from childhood a strong and enthusiastic swimmer, felt that there was no better exercise than an invigorating swim for starting the day. And it was with this thought in mind that he awoke at the crack of dawn, feeling refreshed following a restful night, on New Year's Day, 1967. He wondered what the coming year would bring but was optimistically hopeful in relation to the year ahead.

Alban began his daily ritual by getting into his swimming shorts, slipping into slippers and, with towel in hand, made his way to the nearby beach, while the rest of the family was still in slumber. On arrival at the beach, Alban inhaled deeply and braced himself, before diving into the cool waters. It had been the customary procedure.

Meanwhile, the family awoke expecting to see "Uncle" sitting at the table with a cup of coffee in hand. It had been routinely the case that Alban returned from his daily dip before they were even out of bed, but his well-worn favourite chair was notably empty on that particular New Year's morning. The family were immediately alarmed. They sensed that something was dreadfully wrong and set out to find the much-loved husband and father. It was to no avail. The relevant Services were called and resulted in Alban's life-less body being hauled up from beneath the waves. The discovery was a heart-breaking shock to family and friends in St Vincent, Grenada and beyond. Vincentians who had taken their Grenadian brother into their hearts, were devastated as news of the tragic drowning cascaded across the land. It would also make headline news and was broadcast throughout the region.

An inquest was subsequently carried out into Alban's untimely passing. But even though it was established that Alban's lungs did not contain water, a conclusive cause of drowning was not determined.

The various possibilities that may have led to Alban's misfortune were discussed and debated by family members, friends and interested persons during the following years. Had

Alban been overtaken by strong currents, having ventured too far out at sea? Was he rendered incapacitated by crippling cramp, a stroke, a heart attack, or intoxication. There would never be a definitive answer, and the drowning of Alban Radix may be forever shrouded in mystery.

There can be no denying that Alban's unwavering belief in himself and in his capabilities had been significant factors that contributed towards his achievements. But Alban was also a big-hearted man who cared deeply about other people's welfare and extended a helping hand by doing everything within his means to improve lives and open doors.

Grenadian-born Alban Radix is being classified a historical figure in his beloved adopted country, St Vincent, not only for his humanitarian contributions, but also his landmark successes as a lawyer.

Alban Radix
1917 - 1967

YOU LIVE ONLY ONCE

Lincoln was sitting on a bench at the School House and in the process of filling in a form required for joining the local Scout group. Lincoln quickly wrote down answers to questions such as his name, age and address. Further down the one-page form had been a section requiring information on his parents. Again, no problem. The information was all at his fingertips, until his eyes fell on a specific question. What is the occupation of your mother? Lincoln pondered for a while and, in a "light-bulb" moment of madness, chuckled quietly and in bold letters entered the words: "Child Beater". Lincoln had been well aware that his mother, Angie, was not an official "Child Beater", but felt that it was an apt description for a woman who frequently and mercilessly used the whip for chastising her children. Furthermore, Lincoln was being particularly singled out because of his precocious interest in girls and persistent failure at school. Lincoln seemed to thrive on the thrill of "the dare"; but, through it all, he remained a humorous and fun-loving character with a cheery facial expression, complete with twinkling eyes.

After submitting the completed form, Lincoln sat back with arms folded across his chest and giggled as he anticipated his mother's reaction on reading the form. But he didn't care. What's one more beating? His flesh had already been hardened to the infliction of pain. Consequently, Lincoln may have been surprised and possibly a little disappointed by the absence of parental response but was happy to have been accepted as a member of the Movement alongside his brothers. Participation in the structured environment of Scout activities did not, however, bring about changes in Lincoln's precarious behaviours. Indeed, he may have felt like "the cat who got the cream" when he succeeded in charming an attractive young teacher into initiating him into the sex act. It resulted in an increased inability to concentrate in the classroom, as Lincoln could think of nothing but the next passionate encounter and was intoxicated by the associated risks.

Despite the challenges, Lincoln was a friendly and helpful child, and was often the first among the siblings to volunteer to assist with any required task. William and Angie Radix ensured that their offspring received the educational foundation they hoped would propel them into future separate career objectives. And both parents had been pleased that, apart from Lincoln, the siblings had lived up to expectations by progressing satisfactorily with their school work. In spite of the efforts applied, Lincoln did not advance from basic reading and writing, and showed little interest in even opening a book. It was eventually concluded that "the boy" was just not academically gifted and that nothing could be done about it. He was, on the other hand, strong and capable and never shied away from hard manual work. As a consequence, William and Angie were resigned to the probability that this particular son had been "cut out" for ploughing the field. However, "someone has to do it", and if it's going to be Lincoln, so be it.

Hope had been abandoned that Lincoln would at some point make the required progress at school, and there were no signals of an impending significant turn-around. Everyone was therefore taken by surprise when, without prompting, Lincoln decided to apply himself academically, and in due course progressed from being the "class dunce" to being named highest achiever of his year. Angie was, in equal measure, astonished and delighted that Lincoln had gone on to excel in the school-leaving examinations of the period but bemoaned the fact that William had not lived long enough to witness their son's remarkable turn-around. "He would have been so proud," she said sadly.

Angie was fully supportive when Lincoln disclosed his ambition to become a Pharmacist. The choice of career had been an endorsement of his unexpected but significant transformation. Lincoln would not, as previously envisaged, earn his living by working the field. It had been, for Angie, a moment of immense relief.

Lincoln breezed through Pharmaceutical training and passed out with a mark of distinction. "The boy had done well", and the family were elated. In very little time, after returning home, Lincoln realised the goal of being offered employment in his chosen field, at the local pharmacy. In keeping with his newly acquired occupation, Lincoln decided that having a wife by his side would enhance his image and chose a friendly and bubbly girl named Vera to be his bride. He felt comfortable with Vera and, furthermore, she was loved and fully accepted by Angie and the rest of the family.

Following the marriage, Lincoln appeared to have settled into happy domesticity and, in conjunction with his career, had found fulfilment and stability. Appearances can, however, be deceptive. Even though Lincoln was a caring husband and a doting father to the couple's new-born son, he was also emotionally restless and may have struggled with the constraints of married life. Importantly, also, Lincoln's pharmaceutical interests had faded. He hungered for broader opportunistic experiences and decided to take his career to the next level by applying for entry into a Medical School in the United States.

Angie reeled with amazement on hearing of Lincoln's intention to climb further up the career ladder. She found herself recalling a time when Lincoln had been judged a classic "dunce", due to his failures at school and overall disinterest in learning and was now wondering whether he was just "lazy-minded" or simply a late developer. She would never know the answer, but there could be no denying that Lincoln had proved everyone wrong and that he was far from being intellectually stunted. Lincoln's wife, Vera, was saddened that she would be temporarily parted from her husband just two years into their marriage. But she was supportive of his decision to study abroad and felt reassured in the knowledge that the family would, in the long term, reap benefits.

Both Angie and her daughter-in-law, Vera, were with Lincoln on his departure, and tearfully waved him goodbye. Little did they know that neither would again lay eyes on the beloved son and adored husband.

Although Lincoln received financial assistance from his brothers and sisters, he also took on casual work as a means of supporting himself during the years spent in Medical School. Lincoln's latent appetite for learning and recently discovered drive to succeed resulted in the avoidance of all unnecessary distraction as he focused on his studies. After sailing through set assignments over several years, he had completed the theoretical requirements and was in the process of his internship at a local hospital when he received a telegram informing him that his mother, Angie, was critically ill. However, just prior to booking an airplane ticket to be by her side, he received a second telegram containing crushing news of her passing. In his desire to be a pallbearer at the funeral, Lincoln caught the very next available flight, but landing was delayed due to unusually bad weather. Lincoln would be bitterly disappointed. Not only did he not see his mother again, following the fateful day of his departure to the United States, but his arrival home was later than expected, and, as a consequence, he missed her funeral. He was crestfallen.

At some point following his departure, Lincoln's wife Vera took the decision to move to New York with the couple's toddler son. Vera's mother, who had emigrated to the city several years previously, was happy to be joined by her daughter and little grandson. Furthermore, it had been comforting for Vera to be residing in the country in which her husband had been studying. Even though Lincoln was based many miles away, in Washington DC, Vera clung to the hope that he would one day visit his family in New York. But even though she received no communication from her husband, Vera was convinced that Lincoln had been fully occupied with his busy schedule of work and study, and would, without doubt, return to the family after accomplishing his goal. It was sadly not to be. Lincoln walked away and never looked back.

During the years subsequent to becoming a Medical Doctor, Lincoln resided and held adjoining surgeries, at one time or the other, in various areas across the land, and also on the sister-islands of Carriacou and Petite Martinique. He viewed his profession as being primarily a vocation and felt privileged to have been in a position to help the sick. In so doing, he attended to everyone, regardless of whether or not they were able to afford the fee. But he was prepared to accept payment in kind, such as freshly reaped fruit and/or vegetables.

Lincoln was not satisfied with being just a doctor. He was restless and career-driven, and his enterprises included the opening of a pharmacy in the city of St George. He also built up a chicken farm and went on to secure lucrative contracts for producing and delivering eggs to hotels, restaurants and retail outlets throughout the island. Horses were his passion, and Lincoln acquired stables for rearing and training horses for racing. Horse racing had been a popular public event of the period. It was held on Bank Holiday weekends, and family and friends looked forward to being in attendance and having a flutter on one or more of "Uncle Lincoln's" horses.

Although Lincoln found great personal satisfaction in realising his various career goals, he was immensely proud that, in so doing, he was able to make a contribution to his community by providing jobs to others. He would in due course receive recognition for his overall service by being awarded an MBE from the Queen.

Apart from his various ventures, Lincoln maintained a keen interest in politics. He was in regular communication with the Island's first Prime Minister, Eric Gairy, and was selected to represent the views of his country on Eastern Caribbean decision-making forums. The saying, "It's not what you know, but who knows you", may have been applicable to Lincoln. He maintained amicable working or friendship relationships with people with "clout" and used these contacts to advantage the aspiration of various up and coming individuals. Although Lincoln was a member of the "elite", he retained his links with ordinary folk. He was approachable, had time for everyone and offered a friendly greeting to all and sundry. Indeed, on purchasing his first television set, Lincoln invited his less well-off friends within the community to join him for the very first viewing. The day arrived and his lounge was gradually filled with invitees anxiously awaiting the "big switch on". They cheered and clapped in anticipation as the screen began flickering. However, the expected images failed to appear and the audience was faced with fast-moving jagged lines, accompanied by ear-piercing buzzing sounds. The viewing was eventually abandoned and guests were compensated with an impromptu evening of socialising, with plenty of food and drink.

Lincoln was an outgoing, effervescent and spirited personality. He enjoyed entertaining friends at his house, and everything required for a fun evening was in place. Although he did not touch alcohol, a bar was installed in the lounge and contained a wide variety of spirits, wines and beer. A large radio/recorder was perched on a cabinet stacked with 1950s

American Du-Wop and Rhythm & Blues records, and party participants were served by at least one attractive young woman, specifically recruited for the purpose.

When it came to women, Lincoln was a seasoned operator. He was gifted with the charm and allure that most women found irresistible. No-one knew better than Lincoln that his "know-how" in "pulling" the ladies had been second to none. Apart from himself, he doubted that any other thirteen-year-old school boy of his era could claim to have seduced a young female teacher into sexual activity. Consequently, the "playboy" badge that had been worn with pride was now being bolstered by power and exploited to the "max". And so it was, in parallel with his career-driven pursuits, Lincoln was driven in his serial pursuit of women; addicted, probably, to the buzz of the chase and thrill of the capture.

In spite of being known as a "player", Lincoln was, nonetheless, considered quite a "catch" by various unattached women. He was, after all, a good-looking bachelor with a respected occupation. Moreover, he drove a big car, lived in a large house and possessed attractive personable attributes. But interested singletons had been oblivious to the fact that, although he appeared to be unattached, Lincoln was in reality a married man who was separated from his wife, and a Catholic who did not believe in divorce. He was, also, acutely aware that he had "roving eyes" and was, as a consequence, not suited to married life. Nonetheless, he was not naïve on the subject and advised that "mutual trust and respect" was fundamental to a successful union. However, many would say that Lincoln had consistently broken professional ethics and, in today's climate, would most certainly have been "struck off" the Medical Register.

Lincoln's string of broken relationships left, in their wake, offspring, several of whom were placed in his custody.

And the family was joined by Alban's Vincentian daughter, subsequent to his death. Lincoln proved to be a committed and responsible single parent who left no stone unturned in ensuring that the siblings in his care received the best possible all-round care within a safe and secure environment. The youngsters were properly fed and clothed, went to the best fee-paying schools, prayed with their father on a nightly basis and attended Sunday Services with him. A kindly but capable woman was employed for managing the household. She was a mothering figure, and the children developed a warm and friendly relationship with her.

In his parental role, Lincoln was described as being easy-going and fun. The siblings felt comfortable in his presence and were often engaged in outdoor activity with him. Even though no strict rules or expectations were being applied, Lincoln's morning greeting was usually followed by the question, "So what are your plans for today?" – indicating that they were expected to be constructively single-minded, even in small ways, on a day-to-day basis. But Lincoln would provide the children in his care with the resources for moving forward and achieving their separate personal aspirations; his only advice being: "Whatever you choose to do in life, try to do it to the best of your ability."

It was evident that Lincoln applied very little pressure on his children when a visiting niece recalled being shown a pile of "love letters" that "Uncle Lincoln" secretly retrieved from one of his son's school bags. "Now I know why he hasn't been doing well at school," Lincoln chuckled, and, with an amused expression painted on his face, handed the small bundle of hand-written notes to the curious young lady. He was, no doubt, at that point, recollecting his own boyhood antics and concluding that this particular apple had not fallen too far away from the tree! However, he was not reprimanded or even informed of the find. Moreover, Lincoln would never disclose to the siblings his awareness that they had been driving his car at night when he was mistakenly believed to be asleep!

Although Lincoln remained in contact with the siblings that were not in his care, he convened family get-togethers on an annual basis. These meetings, which were usually held during the Easter break, were filled with a variety of activities, including board games. The siblings would update each other and their father on significant personal developments, and there was always plenty of food and jollies.

After many years of being apart, Lincoln's child from his marriage, Clive, who lived with his mother in New York, was flown over for a lengthy visit with his father. The pair at that stage hardly recognised each other. In particular, the one-time little boy had grown into a young adult. Nonetheless, father and son attempted to get to know each other again by talking and spending quality time together. During the period spent on the island, Clive would for the first time meet with his younger brothers and sisters, and was welcomed with much affection by his aunts, uncles and cousins. Lincoln did everything possible to ensure that his son's visit was not only enjoyable but also beneficial to their relationship. He was not disappointed.

Lincoln was, at heart, a family man. He never lost touch with his brothers and sisters, even those who lived abroad. The siblings maintained a strong bond, and even though they lived separate lives, were at all times supportive of each other and their respective family members.

Lincoln, who was artistically gifted, was often spotted drawing on canvases. However, he also enjoyed gardening and kept a variety of animals. Indeed, in an age when vegetarianism was not appreciated, Lincoln was known to purchase a pig for the purpose of "fattening for Christmas". He also nurtured a bee-hive which had been operating as expected. But it was on a whim that Lincoln decided to relocate the settled network of bees and, prior to evaluating the consequences, he marched up to the hive, grabbed it with both hands and proceeded to carry it to an alternative location. It would be a turbulent transition in which his tolerance of pain, ability to remain calm, maintain focus and determination to keep going were simultaneously tested to the limit. Lincoln found himself being attacked by an army of bees, furious that he had disrupted their settlement. They buzzed angrily and noisily around his head, stampeded into his eyes, ears and nose, all the while sustaining a barrage of piercing stings. Lincoln gritted his teeth through it all, kept calm and hurried on. On placing the hive in a new location, Lincoln echoed victorious relief, indicative of winning a war! There was no way he was going to let them beat him. Lincoln had been, from a child, somewhat of a "dare-devil", fearless in taking risks and charged by the stimulus derived from balancing on the edge.

Immediately following his encounter with the bees, Lincoln quickly rid himself of his clothing and rushed into the shower. But, due to a continual irritating itch, he was convinced that a few of his winged enemies had invaded his nostrils and attempted to expel them by frequently blowing his nose. Indeed, Lincoln's nose had been a prominent facial feature and, as a consequence, often the butt of jokes. He was, however, never offended. He giggled along with the jesters but suggested that they should count themselves "lucky" and claimed that at "one time" people got in line and were charged a "fee" for viewing his nose!

Lincoln loved pulling practical jokes on his family. It included targeting those who complained of having a toothache. Clutching a pair of pliers, menacingly poised for yanking out the offending tooth, at any given opportunity Lincoln would playfully chase the terrified complainant around the house.

Lincoln had been carrying on with his family responsibilities and busy work schedule at the time it was reported that a naked girl had been found raped and murdered. As a result of police investigations, four young men were eventually arrested and charged. The nation was abhorred by the heinous crime. Consequently, the subsequent trial by jury was sensationally reported in newspapers of the period and followed with interest. Not surprisingly, the eventual unanimous guilty verdict and announcement that all four men were sentenced to be executed by hanging was met with a collective sigh of relief. It was generally agreed that justice had been done.

In his role as Pathologist at the island's largest hospital based in the city of St George, Lincoln was called upon to certify the deaths. However, he was not prepared for the horrific discovery that the convicted rapists had also been castrated. Despite being seriously repulsed and shaken to the core, Lincoln completed the required tasks and headed for home. But the highly disturbing experience had taken its toll. Lincoln was broken and, within minutes of returning to his house, he collapsed, and a shining light was all of a sudden extinguished. It had been, for him, a challenge too far.

Everyone was stunned by the extraordinary and untimely demise of the much-loved father, brother, uncle, cousin, friend, associate, doctor and entrepreneur.

A spirited multifarious individual, Lincoln was a visionary who did not procrastinate when it came to putting his various ideas into action. He was also an altruistic soul who actively contributed towards improving the lives of those who struggled. Lincoln is being remembered with much love and appreciation, and memories of his humour put a smile on the faces of those who knew him well.

Lincoln Radix
1913 - 1978

UNPRECEDENTED

Doctor John lay groaning on his bed. He had not long returned from Sunday Mass and had complained of being in severe pain and feeling generally unwell. His wife, Eileen, with whom he had been married for forty-five years, was immediately alarmed. "Not like daddy to take to his bed like that," she told herself. He routinely rose from his bed at the crack of dawn and, dressed in the standard white short-sleeved shirt and tie, would attend church on a daily basis and, after returning home for breakfast, would set off to work. But weekends were often spent working on family-owned land in the country, accompanied by one or more of his sons. Eileen now found herself being overwhelmed with feelings of deep concern. She picked up the telephone and alerted eldest son, Denis, also a doctor.

In response, Denis grabbed his medical bag and hastily made his way to the family home. After examining the patient, father and son, with knowing expressions, locked eyes and Denis had no doubt in relation to the preferred treatment. And Denis wasted no time in preparing and administering the first opium injection. It produced the intended effect. John fell into a deep sleep. Meanwhile, Eileen trooped off to the kitchen. "Just making a pot of soup for 'daddy' to have when he wakes up – it will do him good."

"Good idea," Denis replied, but repeated the dosage as soon as his mother's back was turned, and it was at intervals "topped-up". This action resulted in the beloved father and husband being trapped into a peaceful and pain-free slumber from which he would never escape. He simply slipped away. Eileen was flabbergasted, but also bitterly disappointed that the dearly beloved did not have the opportunity of even having a taste of the soup that been specially prepared for promoting his recovery.

Dr John's demise had signalled the end of an era. The nation had never previously, nor since, known anyone of his like. He was one of a kind.

John had been the second surviving son of William and Angie Radix. He was, from childhood, extremely smart and keenly interested in books and reading. Although being one of a large brood of brothers and sisters, John was a loner and spent nearly all of his free periods reading quietly in the family's study. Books appeared to be his closest companions but may also have been the method used for avoiding his mother's wrath. Indeed, both parents applauded the fact that John had been a studious boy and were ecstatic when, at just 13 years of age, he became the youngest ever person on the island to have won a nation-wide scholarship for attending the prestigious Mount St Benedict's Catholic College, based in Trinidad & Tobago.

Following graduation, John returned home and was offered a teaching position. But he wanted more, and within a few years was a student at Howard University, Washington DC, studying medicine.

As a newly qualified Professional Practitioner, in the 1930s, John had made history. He was the first home-grown black Medical Doctor on the island of Grenada and sister isles, Carriacou and Petit Martinique. Despite his pioneering accomplishment, John was at heart a conscientious individual who placed the needs of others before those of himself. He considered his occupation as being primarily a vocation, or even a spiritual calling, and endeavoured to reach out to disadvantaged communities which, at the time, had been afforded very little access to medical care.

After establishing a working career, John was at the stage in his life where he felt the time was right to focus on his personal life. In line with the majority of young unattached men and women, John looked forward to marrying and raising a family. Little did he know, however, that fate had decreed that his search for a wife would be short-lived. On his very first tentative venture into the specific outdoor venue at which young single people seeking suitors were known to visit on a Sunday afternoon, John spotted two beautiful young ladies chattering and intermittently bursting into loud laughter as they strolled side-by-side. He was instantly struck by one of them. John wasted no time acting on his instincts and, after making a few enquiries, made his move by knocking at the front door of the young lady's residence. It was opened by a maid in full apron, but in response to a specific request, John was invited inside and asked to take a seat while waiting to speak to the mistress of the house. Subsequent to mutual introductions, John communicated his wish for permission to befriend a particular daughter. He was informed that the girls, who were full sisters and one year apart in age, were not her biological children. She had adopted them with her husband when they were one- and two-year-old toddlers, following the death of their mother at just 24 years of age. The young mother had been an unsupported single-parent from a poor family who struggled to "make ends meet" by being employed as a maid by the wealthy childless couple fated to become substitute parents to the orphaned girls.

On requesting permission to get to know, on a personal level, the sister of his choosing, the "mother" was delighted the young doctor, immediately deemed "a big catch", had been interested in one of her daughters, but suggested that the older girl should be more suitable for him. John, whose humble and quietly-spoken persona belied an underlying robust and steely character, would have none of it and stuck to his "guns". He knew exactly who he wanted and would eventually have his wish by being enabled to meet with the girl of his dreams. Her name was Eileen Franco.

The courtship between John and Eileen was brief. The seventeen-year-old had been won over by her suitor's dazzling smile, twinkling eyes, kindness and generosity. She felt safe and comfortable in his company and had no doubt that he would look after her well. Moreover, the couple looked forward to seeing each other and enjoyed spending time together. Eileen's mother came to realise that the relationship had clicked and that John was right in picking the younger girl. Consequently, she believed she was acting in her daughter's best interests by suggesting to John that the couple should marry, sooner rather than later. John was fully onboard, and a wedding was soon being planned. Eileen was still only seventeen years of age when she married the man that was destined to be her life partner.

The couple settled happily into married and were delighted by the arrival of their first son Dennis. John and Eileen considered themselves truly blessed when a daughter they named Arlene followed two years later. The enchanting and engaging baby girl developed into an inquisitive and precocious toddler who, out of the blue, "stomped" her parents by declaring that the baby-sitter charged with taking her for walks, had instead been visiting her boyfriend. The two-year old further revealed that she was being left unattended while the baby-sitter and the boyfriend spent time together in "the room"! Not surprisingly, the unexpected shocking disclosure resulted in the prompt dismissal of a once trusted child-minder.

John and Eileen's marital relationship continued to grow and flourish, and happiness ruled the household. Indeed, life could not have been better, and no obstruction had been anticipated when, all of a sudden, the family's perfect world was shockingly turned upside down. Their treasured "little madam", who amused and livened up the household with her cute antics and grown-up outpourings, contracted a fever and within hours was gone. Both parents were left reeling as their hearts were being ripped into pieces. John, in particular, was openly distraught and inconsolable. He blamed himself for being unable to save his daughter and was tortured by feelings of guilt. He was alleged to have "cried and cried" throughout the funeral of his adored daughter.

A child lost could never be replaced. However, in spite of their grief, John and Eileen ensured that the eight children that followed were raised within a happy, secure and stable home environment. Eileen held responsibility for the smooth running of the household, day-to-day routines and managing the family's small army of domestic staff. John remained committed to being a responsible and reliable husband and father, but even though his life revolved mainly around his family and his work, he maintained regular contact with his own closely-bonded brothers and sisters. As an individual, John had been somewhat of a loner who enjoyed his own company. After returning home from work, he would disappear into his bedroom, cigarette in hand, and absorb himself in a book; or puff away contentedly while listening to news or current affairs reports on the radio. He was also interested in sport and enjoyed listening to live broadcasts of major sporting events such as boxing and international cricket.

Although he was a humorous character with a warm smile, John had very few friends outside of home, and his very own sons were his closest "buddies". Indeed, first son, Denis, who was for nearly ten years the only boy in the family, had been taken under his wing while Eileen concentrated on their daughters. The close friendship between father and son was reflected in John's conversations, as it was always "Denis and the children" whenever he referred to his offspring. During periods when John was not working, the pair were often involved in joint outdoor activities, and their free-flowing joyous banter was regularly filled with hilarious jokes told by John. As Denis grew older, he was encouraged to take hold of the steering wheel during car rides with his father and, by the age of 11, was already a competent driver, capable even of manoeuvring large trucks. The six-feet-tall youngster would go on to pass his driving test on his 13th birthday. It had been his first attempt.

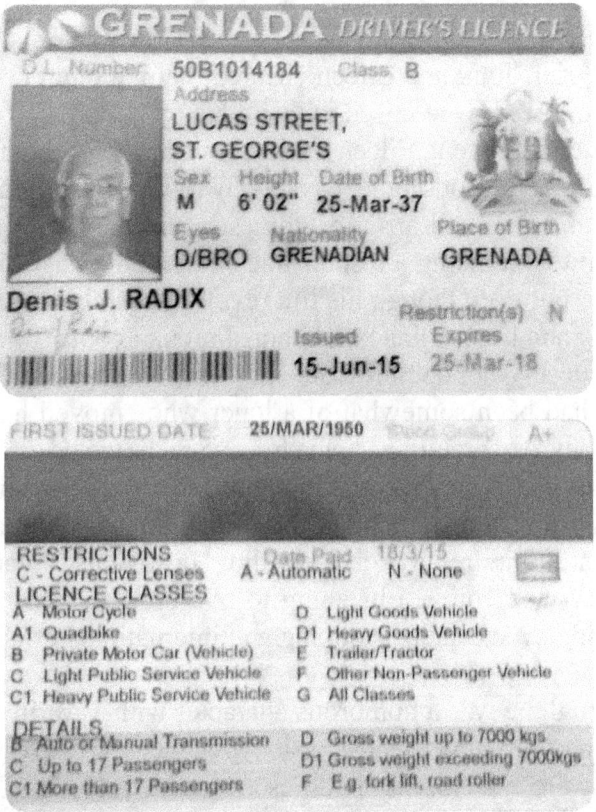

Apart from petrol for his car, John spent only on cigarettes. He was a heavy smoker and avoided the risk of "running out" by pre-ordering them in large quantities. Denis, who was delegated the task of collecting the cartons that contained the ordered items, never ceased to be amazed that, even though his father appeared addicted to tobacco, he abstained from it, totally, during the season of "Lent", and chewed continually on extra-strong mints.

As far as Denis could recall, there was never a time when he did not share a bedroom with his father, even though they slept in separate single beds. His mother, on the other hand, occupied a large double bed in a room of her own. Consequently, the youngster's inquisitive mind would go into free-fall whenever a new baby arrived. He had been aware of how babies were made, but, try as he may, could never work out how it could have happened. But the mystery was eventually solved on the morning Denis awoke to find his father's mattress lying smouldering on the grass outside. John had fallen asleep holding a lighted cigarette, which had at some point fallen onto the sheet and started a fire. The young lad had been completely unaware of the incident or commotion that followed, and all of a sudden realised that "Mummy's" large double bed was not, as he had previously assumed, used solely for coming together as a family in nightly prayer. It was the point at which the pieces of the puzzle slotted into place and the mystery was solved.

Although John was not demonstratively affectionate, Denis never doubted his love. But he cherished the memory of being, for the first and only time he could remember, embraced by the older man. It occurred on the day of Denis's departure to Medical School in Dublin, Ireland. He was at the time 19 years of age.

As Denis grew older and became increasingly independent, he was being replaced by younger brother, Roger, as their father's closest friend. Roger recalled resenting the fact that Denis was always given the "drumstick" whenever chicken was on the menu at mealtime. In those days, chicken leg servings indicated seniority and, as a consequence, were normally placed on the dish of the head of the family, usually the husband, and one other senior member. Roger seethed with a persistent sense of injustice that he was never given a "drumstick". But his emotions were at boiling point on the particular day he decided to defy convention and help himself to the longed-for portion of chicken. On arriving at the table and spotting that his little brother had claimed his "drumstick", Denis was outraged and, without uttering a word, asserted his superiority by promptly leaning over and decisively snatching his rightful possession from Roger's plate. It was an action that in no uncertain terms delivered the message that Roger never forgot. While Denis was around, and when it came to "drumsticks", Roger must always remember his place!

Having been the next in line, Roger naturally replaced Denis by becoming their father's best mate. Roger holds fond memories of meaningful periods spent with John. On weekends, the pair would visit family-owned land in the country, where they collected coconuts that had fallen onto the ground or planted new trees. Roger also accompanied John when he was called to attend to patients in their own homes and would walk behind him, proudly carrying the doctor's bag, most probably with an inflated sense of "little boy" importance. However, the experience may have influenced his future career aspiration, as he was one of four siblings who followed in their father's footsteps.

Like his brother before him, Roger also received motoring lessons and was permitted to drive the family vehicle. On one such occasion, he lost control on approaching a corner at speed and collided with a wall. It resulted in a dented bonnet and shattered windscreen. Roger was shaken but, most of all, feared John's response on being told of the accident. Nonetheless, he "bit the bullet" and bravely confessed after returning home. "Daddy, I damaged the car." There was no response. "Daddy, I damaged the car," Roger repeated.

John puffed long and deep on his cigarette, looked into the eyes of his son and asked, "Anybody injured?"

"No, dad," Roger replied.

"Not to worry," said the relieved father. "We can always get another car."

As with the two older boys, John nurtured not only a parental relationship but also a "pally" friendship with his third son, Peter, and engaged in various outdoor activities with him. But John had been at the same time concerned that his boy was asthmatic and was continually watchful and protective of him. Peter's condition may have magnified regretful recollections concerning the loss of his adored first daughter, and haunting thoughts in relation to "What if?" or "If only". However, John felt that he had been given a second chance, and this time around was determined to avoid all potential risks. John's vigilance involved Peter being required to be at his father's side during family trips and also in church. Peter looked forward to sitting beside his father when the family attended Sunday Mass and, in particular, being moved by John's tuneful and melodic tones that harmonised with the choir. It seemed unbelievable to young Peter that the glorious sounds were actually coming from his father and reaffirmed the fact by periodically staring upwards at his face and reading the movements of his lips. The exquisite spiritual moments would be always remembered.

As a parent, John was kind, considerate and unconditionally generous. He was an excellent provider who ensured that the overall needs of his wife and children were being fully met. But, despite being flexible and empathetic, the paternal head of the family carried a big psychological stick and would strike terror in the hearts of anyone who crossed the line with a cold hard stare, a warning glance or a formidable frown. His daughter, Cynthia, recalled as a teenager returning home from an evening out with friends, much later than expected. Assuming that the family were all asleep, she opened and shut the front door quietly, with the intention of tip-toeing quietly to her bedroom, when she looked up, only to face her father. John was sitting on a chair facing the door, and, without saying a word, penetrated her very being with a glare so profoundly austere that she was left quivering in her shoes and rooted to the spot. After several minutes, John rose from his chair, turned his back on his daughter and walked away. The psychological scolding delivered was never forgotten and the mistake was not repeated.

Despite dabbling briefly into politics by joining his brother Daniel's political campaigns and, on various occasions, being appointed the island's Acting Governor, John remained committed to his work in the community and found considerable personal satisfaction from helping others. Dressed in his customary white shirt and tie, John attended daily surgeries in different areas throughout the land, and for periods of time served communities on the sister isles of Carriacou and Petite Martinique. Many flocked to his surgeries, and he was reputedly compassionate and sympathetic in his manner of approach. Those who attended his surgeries were made to feel at ease, and the endearment, "dear", was regularly used in his communications with female patients. Importantly, each individual was treated with respect and was valued. No-one was turned away, regardless of whether or not they were able to afford the attendance fee or cost of appropriate medications, that were always to hand and delivered on the spot. However, payment in kind, such as raw produce, was never declined. Moreover, the kindly doctor did not hesitate to provide financial assistance to patients who pleaded abject poverty, and even contributed towards the educational fees of various aspiring students from disadvantaged families. Significantly, John did not believe in offering loans, his expressed view being: "If you lend money, don't expect to get it back" – and he simply handed out cash for deserving causes.

John never failed to respond, day or night, to emergencies by attending to patients and providing medicines in the private surgery that adjoined the family home. It was not unusual, however, that individuals declared an inability to pay for the service only after it was delivered. On one such occasion, when he had been woken from his bed in the middle of the night by a seriously ill woman who declared that she had no money, John responded calmly, but asked: "How are you going to get home?"

"Walk, doctor," came the reply.

"You're in no fit condition to walk," said John, and promptly called a cab and paid the driver to transport the patient to her house.

Widely known as "Doctor Dear", John had been, in his era, the best-known and most popular medical practitioner on the islands of Grenada, Carriacou and Petite Martinique. And he was simultaneously humbled and proud to have been awarded an MBE by Her Majesty, the Queen of England, for his charitable services. His greatest reward, however, had been the appreciation he received from ordinary folk.

Apart from relatively short periods when John and his wife travelled abroad and visited close family members who resided in the United States and England, John worked continually for over forty years. But it had been the beginning of the end when, on a particular Wednesday morning, he telephoned his oldest son. John informed Denis that he had taken the decision to discontinue the prescribed medication he had been taking for an incurable prostate problem. He added that his affairs had been placed in order and that it included provisions for "the children". There was no doubt in Denis's mind that he had clearly understood and correctly interpreted the message conveyed by his father.

John attended his surgeries each day subsequently, but, on Sunday morning, Denis was alerted by his mother that John had taken to his bed after returning from church. He responded by hurrying to his father's side but did not disclose the recent conversation with his father. He simply proceeded to initiate the process of ensuring that John experienced a pain-free, comfortable and restful transition. He had been all the while fully aware that it was highly unlikely that John would partake of the soup that was being specifically prepared for him. Eileen, on the other hand, remained hopeful as she waited at her husband's bedside in anticipation that he would, at any moment, rouse from his slumber. It was not to be. She would subsequently conclude that he "just slept and slept and never woke up". Eileen was, nonetheless, happy that his end had been peaceful. John indicated foresight when he said that one of the rewards for a long and happy marriage was having someone by your side when you become old and sick. His prophecy was realised.

The death of Dr John Radix was announced on radio and television and headlined in national newspapers across the region. He was mourned not only by close family members, relatives and friends, but also by an entire nation. Even so, his demise had been personally orchestrated and occurred at a time of his choosing. "Better to wear away than rust away" had been John's expressed opinion.

Dr John led a self-less life. He was essentially an altruistic and magnanimous soul, dedicated to serving his people. He will be forever missed.

John Radix
1904 - 1979

PRINCIPLED MAN

Doreen Williams, a British-qualified State Registered and Psychiatric Nurse, lived and worked in St David's parish during the 1980s, and was among the protestors on the fateful day, 19th October, 1983. She recalled: "A large number of women gathered together. We made banners and posters that read: 'NO WORK. NO SCHOOL, UNTIL BISHOP IS RELEASED'. I held one that said: 'FREE BISHOP. FREE OUR LEADER'. We marched to the city of St George and, during the journey, were joined by large numbers of protestors from parishes across the island. They included people of various ages, young and old and secondary school students, all beating drums and chanting, 'FREE BISHOP. FREE OUR LEADER. FREE HIM NOW'.

"We were among thousands who would subsequently storm into the house in which Bishop was being detained and set him free. The masses were jubilant and collectively went into song by tunefully bellowing, over and over again: "This is our leader", "We find our leader", while marching victoriously with their liberated Head of State towards Fort Rupert, a well-known historical hill that plateaued. On arrival, Bishop addressed his supporters and spoke of his plans for the future and, in particular to 'put right what had gone wrong'."

Meanwhile, Beverley Renwick, a resident of St George's City, had been joyous, having, only moments previously, passed her driving test at the very first attempt. But her joy was unexpectedly replaced with alarm when she spotted three armoured tanks, filled with soldiers, carrying "long guns" similar to "AK 47s". The men were alleged to have had weird "spaced out" expressions as the vehicles progressed steadily "in the direction of Fort Rupert".

Blissfully unaware that troops were on their way, Bishop and his loyal subjects had been in optimistic mood as they stood on the plateau overlooking the sea and euphorically anticipated the bright future that lay ahead.

Doreen Williams picks up the story. "Suddenly and without warning, shooting started on my right. There was great panic as people sought desperately to escape. I suddenly noticed that we were surrounded by tanks and I thought: 'Oh, God, we are going to be killed.' I prayed silently. A young Military pointed his gun at us and said: 'Get out! Get out, for God's sake!' We ran down the hill as fast as we could."

Roger Radix was among local individuals who were alerted to the on-going catastrophe by the horrific sight of bodies "tumbling" off the hill-top and into the sea, on a background of noises that sounded like "fire-crackers".

It was subsequently alleged that Bishop and several others were put up against a wall for some-time before being executed by a firing squad. Roger Radix would for a considerable period, thereafter, experience distressing flashbacks.

The nation was officially informed of the unprecedented tragic events on Radio Free Grenada's 6pm news broadcast, that very day – 19th October 1983. It was announced that Maurice Bishop and three members of his Cabinet had been shot dead. A large number of people were also killed, some of whom perished from falling or jumping over the cliff. The country was now being run by the RMC (Revolutionary Military Council). The nation was stunned and shocked to its very core.

It was evident that, whilst Bishop had been in full flow and his elated followers were wildly cheering their responses to his positive and uplifting messages, the grassy plateau at the top of a hill on which they stood instantly became a killing field. And a dark cloud descended.

One of those personally affected by the tragedy was Lloyd Radix. His son, Kendrick, had been a member of the ruling Cabinet and also a close friend of Maurice Bishop. The men studied Law in London and returned to the homeland in 1970 with a shared political vision.

In 1972, Maurice Bishop, Kendrick Radix and others formed the MAP (Movement for the Assemblies of the People).

In 1973, the MAP merged with the nationally recognised St David's-based political movement known as the JEWEL and formed the NJM (National Jewel Movement).

The 1970s had been a decade of political unrest on the island. Numerous anti-Gairy demonstrations were being violently put down and one such protest, in January 1974, resulted in the fatal shooting of Rupert Bishop, father of Maurice. The political turbulence of the decade culminated in the NJM seizing power in a bloodless coup on 13 March 1979 and forming a revolutionary government. The Prime Minister, Eric Gairy, was, at the time of the coup, out of the country, having left for the United States the previous day, 12th March 1979.

On 21st March 1979, the newly-formed PRG (People's Revolutionary Government) was recognised by Cuba, Guyana and Jamaica. And, despite reservations relating to its leftist orientation, the PRG was recognised by the United Kingdom and United States Governments between 22nd and 24th March 1979.

Maurice Bishop was subsequently appointed Prime Minister under People's Law No. 11 on 29th March 1979.

Now, just four years following what had been a welcomed take-over of power, Lloyd was holding his head in despair and burdened with the belief that his son's action had triggered a revolution.

On 15th October 1983, four days prior to the shootings, Lloyd's son Kenrick convened a public meeting. He informed the people that Bishop had been placed under house arrest and, in passionate tones, called for his release. Kenrick's uncompromising hard-line demands resulted in his prompt arrest and he was placed in police custody. The ramification was that people across the country decided to take matters into their own hands, and free their leader. Ironically, Kenrick would most certainly have been among the consequential fatalities if he had not been in custody on the historic fateful day. Despite being deeply impacted, Lloyd could not help feeling somewhat relieved that Kenrick, by a remarkable twist of fate, had escaped with his life.

The nation was still reeling in shock when, on 25th October 1983, Grenada was under bombardment from a large US military force. The intervention had been in response to a request for assistance from the United States Government. However, the people cowered in fear and hearts thumped as bombs rained down and exploded around them. A significant number of innocent lives, including sixteen patients at the island's largest psychiatric hospital, were lost during the invasion. It was subsequently disclosed that the mental facility had been hit by a 500-pound bomb, after being mistaken for a military installation base.

On 30th October 1983, six thousand United States and Caribbean Military personnel gained full control of the island, and those suspected of involvement in the shootings were arrested and placed in custody. An interim Leader of Grenadian Heritage was appointed the following day, 31st October.

The majority of the United States force would withdraw from the island by 13th December 1983. But even though the overall climate had calmed considerably, Lloyd remained concerned that his son, Kenrick, would continue his political activity.

As a parent, Lloyd had been steadfast in his quest of moulding his two boys into being high achievers in adult life and, from an early age, the boys were subjected to a harsh and uncompromising, testing regime. Lloyd had no regrets. He was satisfied that his efforts had not been in vain. His sons, Michael and Kenrick, went on to accomplish the desired career outcomes and he was proud of them both. Indeed, before the historic deadly uprising of 19th October 1983, Lloyd had been at a contented stage in his life. His offspring had flown the nest and he was enjoying the company of his wife, Eileen, on their various foreign trips, which included visits to his siblings who lived abroad. He would also follow and support the West Indies cricket team during international tours. Nonetheless, Lloyd did not fully retire and returned to his practice following periods of absence.

Lloyd's story began more than seventy years prior to 19th October 1983. He was the third son born to William and Angie Radix and was, from childhood, a single-minded, intelligent and assertive character who devised ways of gaining the attention of his parents. Unlike his siblings, Lloyd did not shy away from their tyrannical and domineering matriarch. Angie was softened by Lloyd's caring overtures and insistence on protecting her whenever William was out of the country, by sleeping in the marital bed. But Lloyd was also at William's side at any given opportunity and offered to assist him with various tasks. As time went on, father and son developed a unique bond and considered themselves "best friends".

All the while, Lloyd had been performing well at school, and both parents were proud that he had completed his education, having achieved excellent grades. Lloyd went on to accept a teaching position, but resigned when the family came into financial difficulties. Always a dutiful son, Lloyd's priority was bolstering the family's income by working overseas alongside his father and brothers when William's once-flourishing business had gone into liquidation. Lloyd would, at some point subsequently, take over responsibility for being the family's main breadwinner, following William's passing. Although he was not the oldest son, Lloyd had been convinced, from an early age, that he was rightfully his father's heir.

The family circumstances improved with time, but Lloyd only returned home on the insistence of his mother, Angie. He went on to resume his teaching career, but before too long had departed to Dental School in the United States. After a period of focused studying, supported by part-time employment, Lloyd accomplished his professional aspiration. He was welcomed back home with joyous celebration. Lloyd went on to open a Dental Practice in the city of St George, but he would fall under the spell of Eileen Arthur, at the time considered one of the most attractive and sought-after young ladies within the locality. The couple married and over ensuing years produced four children: two sons followed by two daughters.

The family resided, for a time, on the island of Trinidad, where Lloyd also operated a practice. They returned permanently to the homeland following the demise of his beloved mother, Angie.

Lloyd was at all times well-groomed and smartly attired, but his often stern and intimidating presence masked an underlying caring and helpful spirit who desired better for others. Despite this fact, Lloyd had been firmly of the view that everything in life comes with a price tag. Consequently, patients who were unable to afford the required fee were given no anaesthetic prior to treatment. The sensation of pain may have been the alternative cost demanded. However, Lloyd reached out by providing employment to school leavers from disadvantaged homes and several were trained to become Dental Technicians. He also provided financial assistance to those who were proved to be trying, but struggled to acquire a home of their own.

Although his children had been born into a privileged class, Lloyd strived to ensure that they did not become selfish individuals who believed they were entitled or even better than those who were less fortunate. And they were not reprieved from his "no free lunches" principles. Consequently, whenever the brothers asked for something specific or even permission to participate in a leisure activity with their peers, Lloyd never failed to respond with the question, "What have you done for the day?" Any hesitation would be met with harsh directions, such as, "Go and clean the car!", "Sweep the yard!" or "Feed the dog!" Moreover, pocket money had to be seen to be earned before it was ever given.

Lloyd's sons were placed in the best fee-paying Secondary Boys' School of the day and their performance was closely monitored. Nevertheless, they were, at the end of each school day, delivered additional work by their father and punished with a single stinging stroke of the belt on their backside for each mistake made. The threatening of physical chastisement often resulted in two highly intimidated boys being mentally paralysed and unable to focus, resulting in an increased number of inaccuracies and corresponding lashes. But Lloyd was determined to continue the *status quo*. He was certain that his uncompromising methods would, in the long term, reap benefits.

Lloyd's rigid stance in relation to education was also extended to his nephews. He regularly visited the family homes of his brothers and sisters, and the respective siblings would be required to hand over their text books for inspection. Any errors, inconsistencies or shoddiness detected would be penalised with the belt. Consequently, whenever he was spotted approaching, the panic-stricken youngsters would alert each other by nervously exclaiming, "Uncle Lloyd coming! Uncle Lloyd coming!", as they scattered in fear while attempting to conceal themselves from the punitive relative.

One particular day, Lloyd returned home from his office to find a youth tending to the area surrounding the family home. Lloyd was immediately taken aback and asked, "What are you doing?"

"Yuh wife hire me to do de job – sar," the lad humbly replied.

Lloyd was flabbergasted. "I have two fat sons in the house – and you are hired to work? Put that rake down and come with me!" Lloyd demanded. He led the young man into the house, offered him a seat and a cool drink, before raging at his strapping, well-nourished boys, "Michael! Kenrick! You are two lazy fat slobs! Get out there at once and start cleaning the yard. Right now!"

Although there could be no denying his robust discipline, Lloyd was a devoted and responsible husband and father. He was at all times known to use the endearing term "honey" when referring to the mother of his children, and would affectionately pick up his daughters and sit them on his lap. He engaged in outdoor activities with his boys, and in particular enjoyed participating in a game of cricket. He also taught them to drive as soon as they entered their teenage age. On a personal level, Lloyd socialised with longstanding friends, and on those occasions was alleged to have been the life and soul of the party: jovial, happy-go-lucky, with plenty of jokes to tell.

Lloyd's home was his castle. He loved being surrounded by beautiful furnishings in an environment enhanced with exquisite tanks filled with exotic fish. Lloyd derived a sense of peace from the different sizes and varieties of colourful tropical fish as they swam furiously or simply floated on the water within their habitat. But he was also at times considered a reclusive. Lloyd had been known to occupy a separate bedroom from his wife, but may, for several hours, retreat quietly into his own private space.

Lloyd was both relieved and happy that eldest son, Michael, had finished school having obtained the required GCE results for being accepted into higher education in Canada. Lloyd had been of the opinion that Michael could be relied upon to handle, independently, the cash for meeting the carefully calculated expenses during the proposed year-long period of study. But, nonetheless, he delivered clear instructions on how the funds should be budgeted.

On arrival at his destination and for the first time being in the possession of a considerable amount of money, caution was thrown to the wind and Michael decided to treat himself to a spending spree. He booked into a hotel, purchased a small car and for a while lived lavishly. On realising that cash had disappeared before he had even paid the semester fee, Michael took pen to paper and wrote to his father requesting a top-up. Lloyd's reply was swift and brief: "Not my concern. Get on with it! Dad." Michael had no choice but to find various jobs and even pawned some of his possessions in order to pay for college fees, basic accommodation and food.

Despite Lloyd's refusal to provide additional funds to his son, Michael's efforts resulted in success. He subsequently entered Medical School in Dublin, Ireland, but Lloyd had learnt a lesson from his son's previous mis-handling of cash money and, as a consequence, university fees were paid direct, while Michael received a monthly allowance. Everything appeared to be running smoothly, but within months Lloyd received a letter from his son stating that a local girl was expecting his baby and that he needed to have his personal allowance increased. Lloyd was outraged and replied promptly, "Sorry, but that is your problem. Not mine. You got yourself into it, so, Good Luck! Dad." A year followed and Lloyd received a subsequent letter from Michael informing him that he had decided to get married, as his girlfriend was having their second child. The response had been once again short and very much to the point: "Guess you need even more luck, now. Dad."

Although disappointed by his father's seemingly lack of empathy or compassion, alongside his studies, Michael had a family to support and spent every hour during free periods working at whichever job he could find. But he would be forever indebted to his cousin, Cynthia, also at the time a medical student in Ireland, for her generous financial assistance.

Despite several years of juggling studying with work and family commitments, Michael won through in the end and Lloyd was elated. And though Michael had secured employment as a General Practitioner in Dublin, Lloyd rewarded his son by continuing to pay his monthly allowance for one year subsequent to qualification.

Lloyd experienced no headache from his second-born son, Kenrick, when he studied Law in London. Even though he also received the minimum monthly allowance, while university fees were being paid direct, Kenrick did not give in to distraction, and, as a consequence, made no additional demands on his father. But he was remunerated by the older man's joy and declaration of pride in his eventual success.

As adults, Michael and Kenrick both acknowledged that Lloyd was never demonstratively affectionate towards them. However, the brothers dearly loved their "dad", and neither doubted that he loved them back. It was also their expressed opinion that their father meant well, even though his harsh discipline methods may have been "wrong". But Lloyd had worked hard throughout his life. Everything he acquired in life had been earned and appreciated, and he was resolute in passing these values on to his sons. Consequently, there could be no doubting that Lloyd would have been convinced that his "tough love" approach had been "right".

Despite the fact that he had not fully recovered from the shocking events of 19th October 1983, Lloyd moved on with his life. He attended his practice on a daily basis, maintained a loving relationship with his wife and family, enjoyed looking after and admiring his array of treasured fish and generally made the best of life.

Less than a year had passed after that historic fateful day, and Lloyd was in the process of treating a patient, when he suddenly fell ill. He was escorted to his house by a member of his staff and assisted into bed. A medic was called by his concerned wife, Eileen, but as she sat by her husband's side and waited anxiously for the doctor to arrive, Lloyd looked into her eyes and uttered his last words: "Honey, hold my hand," he pleaded. She obliged, lovingly, and he drifted peacefully into forever slumber.

Lloyd is being remembered with much love and respect by his family, friends, and those to whom he offered a helping hand. He was a tough nut to crack, but, nonetheless, a well-meaning man with strongly-held views. He was, undeniably, a principled man.

www.ingramcontent.com/pod-product-compliance
Lightning Source LLC
Chambersburg PA
CBHW071454080526
44587CB00014B/2099